DUNGEONS & DRAGONS AND PHILOSOPHY

The Blackwell Philosophy and PopCulture Series

Series editor William Irwin

A spoonful of sugar helps the medicine go down, and a healthy helping of popular culture clears the cobwebs from Kant. Philosophy has had a public relations problem for a few centuries now. This series aims to change that, showing that philosophy is relevant to your life – and not just for answering the big questions like "To be or not to be?" but for answering the little questions: "To watch or not to watch *South Park*?" Thinking deeply about TV, movies, and music doesn't make you a "complete idiot." In fact it might make you a philosopher, someone who believes the unexamined life is not worth living and the unexamined cartoon is not worth watching.

Already published in the series:

24 and Philosophy: The World According to Jack
Edited by Jennifer Hart Weed, Richard Brian Davis, and Ronald Weed

30 Rock and Philosophy: We Want to Go to There
Edited by J. Jeremy Wisnewski

Alice in Wonderland and Philosophy: Curiouser and Curiouser
Edited by Richard Brian Davis

Arrested Development and Philosophy: They've Made a Huge Mistake
Edited by Kristopher Phillips and J. Jeremy Wisnewski

The Avengers and Philosophy: Earth's Mightiest Thinkers
Edited by Mark D. White

Batman and Philosophy: The Dark Knight of the Soul
Edited by Mark D. White and Robert Arp

Battlestar Galactica and Philosophy: Knowledge Here Begins Out There
Edited by Jason T. Eberl

The Big Bang Theory and Philosophy: Rock, Paper, Scissors, Aristotle, Locke
Edited by Dean Kowalski

The Big Lebowski and Philosophy: Keeping Your Mind Limber with Abiding Wisdom
Edited by Peter S. Fosl

Black Sabbath and Philosophy: Mastering Reality
Edited by William Irwin

The Daily Show and Philosophy: Moments of Zen in the Art of Fake News
Edited by Jason Holt

Downton Abbey and Philosophy: The Truth Is Neither Here Nor There
Edited by Mark D. White

Dungeons & Dragons and Philosophy: Read and Gain Advantage on All Wisdom Checks
Edited by Christopher Robichaud

Ender's Game and Philosophy: The Logic Gate is *Down*
Edited by Kevin S. Decker

Family Guy and Philosophy: A Cure for the Petarded
Edited by J. Jeremy Wisnewski

Final Fantasy and Philosophy: The Ultimate Walkthrough
Edited by Jason P. Blahuta and Michel S. Beaulieu

Game of Thrones and Philosophy: Logic Cuts Deeper Than Swords
Edited by Henry Jacoby

The Girl With the Dragon Tattoo and Philosophy: Everything is Fire
Edited by Eric Bronson

Green Lantern and Philosophy: No Evil Shall Escape this Book
Edited by Jane Dryden and Mark D. White

Heroes and Philosophy: Buy the Book, Save the World
Edited by David Kyle Johnson

The Hobbit and Philosophy: For When You've Lost Your Dwarves, Your Wizard, and Your Way
Edited by Gregory Bassham and Eric Bronson

House and Philosophy: Everybody Lies
Edited by Henry Jacoby

The Hunger Games and Philosophy: A Critique of Pure Treason
Edited by George Dunn and Nicolas Michaud

Inception and Philosophy: Because It's Never Just a Dream
Edited by David Johnson

Iron Man and Philosophy: Facing the Stark Reality
Edited by Mark D. White

Lost and Philosophy: The Island Has Its Reasons
Edited by Sharon M. Kaye

Mad Men and Philosophy: Nothing Is as It Seems
Edited by James South and Rod Carveth

Metallica and Philosophy: A Crash Course in Brain Surgery
Edited by William Irwin

The Office and Philosophy: Scenes from the Unfinished Life
Edited by J. Jeremy Wisnewski

Sons of Anarchy and Philosophy: Brains Before Bullets
Edited by George A. Dunn and Jason T. Eberl

South Park and Philosophy: You Know, I Learned Something Today
Edited by Robert Arp

Spider-Man and Philosophy: The Web of Inquiry
Edited by Jonathan Sanford

Superman and Philosophy: What Would the Man of Steel Do?
Edited by Mark D. White

Supernatural and Philosophy: Metaphysics and Monsters… for Idjits
Edited by Galen Foresman

Terminator and Philosophy: I'll Be Back, Therefore I Am
Edited by Richard Brown and Kevin Decker

True Blood and Philosophy: We Wanna Think Bad Things with You
Edited by George Dunn and Rebecca Housel

Twilight and Philosophy: Vampires, Vegetarians, and the Pursuit of Immortality
Edited by Rebecca Housel and J. Jeremy Wisnewski

The Ultimate Daily Show and Philosophy: More Moments of Zen, More Moments of Indecision Theory
Edited by Jason Holt

The Ultimate Harry Potter and Philosophy: Hogwarts for Muggles
Edited by Gregory Bassham

The Ultimate Lost and Philosophy: Think Together, Die Alone
Edited by Sharon Kaye

The Ultimate South Park and Philosophy: Respect My Philosophah!
Edited by Robert Arp and Kevin S. Decker

The Walking Dead and Philosophy: Shotgun. Machete. Reason.
Edited by Christopher Robichaud

Watchmen and Philosophy: A Rorschach Test
Edited by Mark D. White

Veronica Mars and Philosophy
Edited by George A. Dunn

X-Men and Philosophy: Astonishing Insight and Uncanny Argument in the Mutant X-Verse
Edited by Rebecca Housel and J. Jeremy Wisnewski

DUNGEONS & DRAGONS AND PHILOSOPHY

READ AND GAIN ADVANTAGE ON ALL WISDOM CHECKS

Edited by
Christopher Robichaud

WILEY Blackwell

Library of Congress Cataloging-in-Publication Data applied for

Paperback ISBN: 978-1-118-39762-6

A catalogue record for this book is available from the British Library.

Cover image: Illustration by Severino Baraldi (b.1930). Private Collection / © Look and Learn / The Bridgeman Art Library.

Set in 11/14pt Sabon by SPi Publisher Services, Pondicherry, India

1 2014

Contents

Abbreviations Used in the Text

D&D	*Dungeons & Dragons*
DM	Dungeon Master
LARP	live action role-playing
MMORPG	massively multiplayer online role-playing game
NPC	non-player-character
PC	player-character
RPG	role-playing game

Introduction
A Game Like No Other

Forty years. No, I'm not talking about the maximum number of years a ghost can age your PC on a hit. (Half-orcs be warned! Those blows will cost you dearly.) I'm talking about the game. The one that started it all and that promised to be something completely different from anything we'd ever seen before.

> This game lets all your fantasies come true. This is a world where monsters, dragons, good and evil high priests, fierce demons and even the gods themselves may enter your character's life. Enjoy, for this game is what dreams are made of![1]

It's been forty years since Gary Gygax and Dave Arneson gave us the first tabletop role-playing game, *Dungeons & Dragons*. Making its way through the wargaming crowd that Gygax and Arneson navigated, *D&D* quickly grew in popularity. What started as a few white books – if you could even call them that – gave way to the numerous hardbound manuals of *Advanced Dungeons & Dragons*, a series of boxed sets, miniatures, toys, video games, novels, comic books, and a Saturday morning cartoon. Heck, even Steven Spielberg gave *D&D* an oblique shout-out in *E.T. the Extra-Terrestrial*. The first edition was followed by the second, the third, the fourth, and now we are about to embrace the fifth.

Dungeons & Dragons and Philosophy: Read and Gain Advantage on All Wisdom Checks, First Edition. Edited by Christopher Robichaud.
© 2014 John Wiley & Sons, Inc. Published 2014 by John Wiley & Sons, Inc.

Just about everyone I know who's played the game has a story about what got them into it. I owe it all to my uncle, who, one very snowy Christmas Eve, gave me the Red Box and, without exaggeration, changed my life forever. I've been playing *D&D* now for three decades, and I'll stop only when they pry that D20 from my cold, dead hand.

During the 1980s, some people were prepared to do just that. A vocal minority during this time thought that playing *Dungeons & Dragons* would allow you to summon Satan, or gain supernatural powers, or summon Satan while gaining supernatural powers. Just check out Jack Chick's *Dark Dungeons* to get a sense of how that line of "reasoning" went. In retrospect, it's hysterical. But we can't ignore the fact that *D&D* almost suffered a critical hit due to malicious propaganda. And for decades after, the game remained stigmatized.

We're (mostly) past that now, thank goodness, with *D&D* having reached a new level of cultural, dare I say, coolness. Oh, let's not kid ourselves. We're still a bunch of fantasy freaks and gaming geeks, to nod and wink at Ethan Gilsdorf's wonderful book. But the game itself has donned new, shiny armor. With hit television shows like *Community* featuring it and theatrical productions like *She Kills Monsters* celebrating it, *D&D* has defied the odds and crawled out of the Tomb of Horrors triumphant. No small feat!

On the occasion of *D&D*'s fortieth birthday, then, and in light of its heightened cultural position, we have put together this book as a tribute to the rich depths of thinking that playing *D&D* lends itself to. And we're talking *D1-2: Descent Into the Depths of the Earth* kind of depths. All the contributors to this volume love philosophy and love *Dungeons & Dragons* and have brought those passions together to bear considerable fruit, much better than the spell *create food and water* would accomplish.

One final note. I have intentionally kept this volume ecumenical in its attitude to the various editions of the game and its attitude to the various philosophical traditions examining those editions. In short: all are welcome. Just like the best of adventuring parties, we may squabble and pout and poke fun at each other, but at the end of the long day, we're in it together. There's a whole wide world filled with dungeons to explore and dragons to slay out there. So let's get to it. We begin, as, of course, we must, in a tavern...

Note

1.   Gary Gygax, *Player's Handbook* (1978).

Part I

LAWFUL GOOD VS. CHAOTIC EVIL

Sympathy for the Devils
Free Will and *Dungeons & Dragons*

Greg Littmann

The fundamental conflict underlying the worlds of *Dungeons &
Dragons* is that between good and evil. On one side are gods of
good like Pelor and Bahamut, supported by their clerics and
paladins and decent adventurers everywhere. On the other side
are the cruel gods of evil, like the cadaverous Vecna and spidery
Lolth, along with legions of demons and devils, grinning undead,
and ugly, rampaging humanoids. Good-aligned adventurers
know that demons and devils alike must be made to leave the
prime material plane immediately and that the philosophical
differences between the evil-aligned drow and the chaotic evil-
aligned orcs are less significant in the great scheme of things than
the shared evil nature that makes them both so dangerous.

Life is hard when you are born to be bad in *D&D*. The evil-
aligned species of the monster manuals generally live in misery.
Evil humanoids like orcs and goblins spend their lives being
bullied by their peers, before eventually charging to a bloody
death in melee. Intelligent undead are often left for centuries just
staring into space, while evil people not lucky enough to become
undead end up in the Abyss or the Nine Hells, where conditions
are, to be blunt, hellish, as souls are tormented by chain devils or
ripped apart by shrieking vrock. Even being promoted through

the ranks of devils brings no respite – your immediate superiors are always evil bastards, the more so the higher you go. If you think *your* boss is bad, try working for Asmodeus!

Not even the *good* guys show the bad guys any sympathy. A party of good characters will chop and char a tribe of orcs to so much smoking hamburger without the slightest hesitation or regret. Not even the cleric says a few words over the corpses – she's too busy looting them for small change. Likewise, good characters will carve their way through packs of rotting undead and gangs of howling demons and devils without giving a thought to how awful being carved up feels to the monsters, or where the poor blighters end up now and how much worse their next assignment might be.

Why is there so little sympathy for the forces of evil? Presumably, it is precisely *because* they are evil. It is considered justice for bad things to happen to evil people (using the word "people" in its broadest sense, so as to include the various non-human intelligent individuals found in the worlds of *D&D*). Appeals to reciprocity might be made: the orcs we slaughter wouldn't hesitate to slaughter *us* if they ever got the upper hand. The undead hate us just for being alive, while the things the devils would do to us if they had their way would make death in battle look like a merciful release.

How you treat your imaginary enemies doesn't matter in itself. If it pleases you to imagine taking Asmodeus' ruby rod and ramming it up his nose, then you go ahead and imagine that all you like, for all the harm you are going to do anybody. But considering the justification of the moral attitudes of *D&D* characters is philosophically useful because attitudes shown towards combating evil in *D&D* mirror the attitudes that many people take towards combating evil in the *real* world. Whether your make-believe wizard is fulfilling his moral duty to a pretend vampire doesn't matter in itself, but how we treat people we label as "evil" in *this* world does.

Philosophers test moral theories by subjecting them to "thought experiments," hypothetical situations set up and considered in an attempt to decide whether particular moral theories give the right answers in all possible circumstances. *D&D* games are nothing *but* thought experiments, hypothetical situations in which hypothetical people do hypothetical things. Of the various story-telling art forms that can serve as a source for thought experiments, *D&D* is *particularly* suitable because the *D&D* player is an active participant in the story, forced to make decisions based on the situations described by the Dungeon Master.

Pity the Pit Fiend

Why *should* we feel sympathy for the evil-aligned monsters of *D&D*? One factor that might move us is that so many of them seem to be evil by *nature*. That is, they are evil given the very type of being they are. While a corrupt human or malicious halfling might have taken a wrong turn in life, other humanoids like orcs, goblins and trolls, along with non-humanoids like red dragons, ropers, or grell are born to their alignment; a red dragon is an *evil* creature – it says so right in the *Monster Manual*. Of course, the *Monster Manual* also states, "A monster's alignment is not rigid, and exceptions can exist to the general rule,"[1] so beings labeled as "evil" in the manuals don't *necessarily have* to be evil. Your PC *could* meet a red dragon looking to defect to the side of good, or a grell philosopher so tormented by the moral implications of her thought experiments that she can no longer eat people and is wasting away from hunger. But if the probability of a creature being anything other than evil is so slight that it is dealt with by a general disclaimer regarding monster alignment in the front of the *Monster Manual*, then there seems to be something unfair about holding it to blame for *being* an evil creature.

If the overwhelming majority of the members of a species behave a certain way, then either it is an astounding fluke, or something about being a member of that species *explains* that tendency; which is to say that something about being a creature of that type in that environment generally *causes* the associated behavior. Ropers spend their lives killing innocent adventurers to devour their flesh. Either it is an incredible coincidence that ropers are generally found murdering people for a living instead of tilling the soil or running an adventurer's supply shop, or there is something about *being* a roper that explains their murdering behavior; which is to say that something about being a roper *causes* ropers to kill.

Once we can see the external causes of a behavior, we tend to be less willing to blame someone for exhibiting that behavior. It is hard to blame the poor roper for its record of murder and stalactite fraud if it was being born as a roper that caused young Rocky to turn to a life of crime. After all, the roper didn't *choose* to be a roper rather than a half-elf or a dryad; that it was a roper was entirely beyond its control. Likewise, when a glabrezu demon is spawned from the elemental chaos, waving its crab claws and swearing blasphemous and chaotic words, there can be no doubt that the poor bat-headed bastard never had a *choice* about being chaotic evil. As much as we might object to all the pincer violence and foul language, we can't reasonably *blame* the demon for being born a demon.

In fact, nobody can rightly be held to blame for the way they act if they could not have acted any differently. If this principle is in doubt, it can be demonstrated by the following thought experiment. Imagine that you are playing a good-aligned cleric in a dungeoneering party. You are in a dark stone corridor, guarding the rear as the team advances into unknown territory. Out ahead, the rogue is scouting in stealth mode, searching for traps and watching for monsters. Suddenly, the dice hit the table the wrong way and the rogue fails a crucial Perception check. The fighter and paladin take another step forward and there is a loud "click" as the corridor begins to tilt downwards, swiftly becoming a stone slide into a lower-level room filled with fero- cious, slavering ghouls. The floor is dropping so fast that the rogue is the only one to make the roll to stay standing. Unfor- tunately for the rogue, the DM announces that you crash right into her, a cannonball in chainmail, as you slide helplessly toward the pit, and now you and the rogue slide *together* toward the bone-strewn nest of the ravenous dead.

Just when it looks like things can't get any worse, the rogue's player gives you the stink-eye and says "As I slide down, I'm going to take my rapier and stick it in the *cleric*. I'm using *crimson edge* to make sure the wound bleeds for the ghouls." And *then* the DM tells you "I'm revoking all of your clerical powers! There's no way that pushing the rogue into a pit filled with ghouls isn't a major violation of your good alignment. Don't think that Pelor is going to help you *turn* those puppies down there. Pelor thinks you are *ooze*." It seems natural to object "But my cleric couldn't *help* it! Once the trap went off, I fell down and that's when I hit the rogue. You can't blame the cleric – the cleric never had a choice."

Damnation Without a Saving Throw

What makes the evil monsters of *D&D* philosophically interesting is how obvious the connection often is between their evil behavior and factors entirely outside of their control. One second you are raw elemental chaos, the next, a spikey demon who exists to destroy. Like the falling cleric, the predicament of monsters born to be evil illustrates that when we can see the external causes of behavior, we deny that the subject is acting from free will and, if we are being consistent, we withhold moral blame. However, it isn't whether we can clearly *see* the external causes of a behavior that makes the moral difference. The morally important thing is that the behavior *has* external causes – it isn't right to blame someone for something they couldn't help doing. What makes this philosophically interesting is that it means that *nobody* has free will in the morally relevant sense. There is no such thing as free will! We are, all of us, falling clerics pulled helplessly along by natural laws.

After all, our bodies are physical things and physical things always act in strict accordance with the laws of physics. Any alteration in a physical system requires energy, so unless energy comes streaming into the physical universe from outside, there is no force we can *add* to the physical universe in order to make an alteration in what it is already set up to do. Your body is a machine made of meat and giblets, and machines do what their physical structures dictate they do – to do otherwise would be to defy natural law. More specifically, your brain is a fleshy computer, and like any other computer, must act in accordance with the way that it is programmed to act. We have learned enough about the universe to be able to recognize that we are, all of us, golems, slaves to the orders that bind us.

To say that an action is "determined" is to say that the action must occur, given previous events and the laws of nature. Since ancient times, philosophers have worried that if the universe is entirely deterministic – that is, if every event in the universe is causally determined – then free will is impossible. The Roman philosopher Lucretius (99–55 BCE) wrote in his *On the Nature of the Universe*, "If all motion is always one long chain, and new motion arises out of the old in order invariable ... whence comes this free will?"[2] The French philosopher Baron d'Holbach (1723–89) – whose name would be good for an evil warlord – accepted determinism and thus denied free will. He wrote in *The System of Nature*: "All the steps taken by man to regulate his existence, ought only to be considered as a long succession of causes and effects, which are nothing more than the development of the first impulse given him by nature."[3] So, for instance, if you decide to play *D&D* one day instead of going to work, it would have defied the laws of nature for you to decide any other way, given the mechanical structure of your body. You are no more choosing freely when you decide to hack lizardfolk with your friends today than the cleric is choosing freely when he falls in accordance with the law of gravity.

Free Will in the Lair of the Succubus

Many philosophers have denied that there is any incompatibility between having free will and our actions being determined. Appropriately known as "compatibilists," these philosophers generally believe that your actions are *free* if your own preferences play an appropriate role as links in the causal chain that results in your actions. As the English philosopher Thomas Hobbes (1588–1679) put it in his *Leviathan*, "Lastly, from the use of the word *free-will*, no liberty can be inferred to the will, desire, or inclination, but the liberty of the man; which consisteth in this, that he finds no stop, in doing what he has the will, desire, or inclination to do."[4] Thus, your decision to play *D&D* instead of going to work would be free if your *desire* to play *D&D* played a decisive role in the outcome that you *did* play *D&D* – if, for instance, your mad craving to try out a minotaur barbarian was so great that it overcame your fear of poverty and drove you to the gaming table. Even if your decision was already set at the Big Bang, as long as your actions are *in accordance* with your desires, then you are free on this model.

Unfortunately, the compatibilist model of freedom still fails in cases where the causal chain is particularly obvious. For instance, let's say that you are playing a good-aligned fighter, and you are down the old dungeon one day when the party comes across a room containing what appears to be a helpless prisoner chained to the wall. You release her, because that is what good adventurers do, and she turns out to be a succubus, because that is what helpless prisoners in the dungeon are. Correctly guessing that you have the lowest wisdom in the party, the succubus throws her *dominate* at *you*, and takes control of your actions, at which point the DM announces that you turn your back on the devil and use your axe to chop at the party warlock. Once the fight is over and the succubus banished back to Dis to fill out forms, your team-mates turn on *you*, taking the 50 feet of hempen rope from your adventurer's kit and tying a noose in it to hang you with. "You don't *ever* turn against the party!" growls the ranger.

Something seems unfair about the party blaming your fighter in this way. But why? Turning on an innocent person and chopping at them with an axe is an archetypical example of what we would normally call immoral behavior. Note, furthermore, that the fighter was acting entirely in accordance with his desires. Ever since the succubus put the whammy on him, he *wanted* to protect her. When he took a swing at the warlock, it was because he *wanted* to chop him up. People who willingly do such things to other people are reviled as thé worst of the worst. Sometimes they say "The devil made me do it," but this defense rarely gains them any sympathy. Yet in the case we are looking at, the devil really *did* make the fighter do it. She charmed him with her black magic and the DM took control of the character, announcing the attack against the warlock. Because the fighter couldn't help what he did, because no other course of action was open to him, it is unfair to hold him responsible for trying to trim the warlock with an axe.

How Thorin Axebeard Randomly Defended the Bridge

So we cannot be free if our actions are entirely determined. That might make it seem that the possibility of freedom hangs on whether determinism is true or not. If that were so, it would be good news for fans of free will, since it turns out that determinism is *not* true – our universe is not entirely deterministic. According to most popular interpretations of quantum mechanics, sometimes things happen *randomly* at the subatomic level. That is, they do not happen for any previous reason, but instead happen for no reason at all. They are *undetermined*. For example, the rate at which a radium atom will undergo radioactive decay is undetermined. While every element has an average decay rate, an individual atom will decay at random. In principle, undetermined events at the quantum level could influence human behavior. They could direct you to step right or left, or to play a ranger or a warlord, or to make a moral decision one way or the other – to tell the other players about the rune-encircled ring your shaman just found, or to have the character just slip it onto her finger and not mention it. Might this subatomic randomness be freedom? This has been the hope of some philosophers almost from the time Werner Heisenberg (1901–76) published his uncertainty principle in 1927, introducing randomness to quantum theory.

Alas, randomness may rescue us from strict determinism, but acting randomly brings us no more *freedom* than we would have if events were entirely determined. To illustrate, consider the following thought experiment. Your DM introduces some new house rules she's made up, in the form of pages of detailed percentile tables describing the reactions of PCs to the events around them. When your party meets a mysterious black-clad elf on the roadway, you don't trust him and want to steer clear, but the DM rolls a couple of D10s and tells you that the party have graciously asked the sinister elf to tag along. Later, your dwarven fighter is standing at one end of a subterranean stone bridge, having just held off a goblin onslaught to protect the team behind. The corpses of goblin warriors lie piled around his feet, but not one of them made it through. Now a deep horn sounds and the rock trembles as the enemy herd a dark wave of towering ogres to the other side of the bridge to make the next assault. The foe is too strong! You want your dwarf to shout "Retreat!" and make good use of unencumbered speed running back to the surface as fast as he can. But the DM rolls her D10s again and tells you that no, the dwarf is going to charge straight down the bridge at the ogres, dropping his shield and yelling "Death for Moradin!" All night, every single action your character takes is decided entirely by the roll on the DM's tables.

Eventually you object, "You don't need me here. I make no difference at all to what my character does or says or thinks. Thorin Axebeard is nothing but a puppet controlled by your Dwarven Culture and Psychology tables, dancing along to the dice. You aren't giving *me* the freedom to decide what my character does."

"But I am giving you *complete* freedom!" retorts the DM indignantly, holding up the two D10s. "The rolls are effectively random. You can't *get* anything freer than a random result – that's all the freedom there is in the universe. We can either roll dice on my tables or quantum particles in your head to decide what Thorin does, and the role-playing is better when we use my tables." Clearly, though, the DM is *not* giving you the freedom to decide what your character does. When the DM makes your character's actions random, the DM has taken away your control of the character.

Likewise, our actions are not free if we act at random in everyday life, a puppet of the great tables in the sky. So indeterminacy offers no more freedom than determinacy does. One could argue, following the compatibilist, that we are acting freely as long as our actions are caused by our desires, even if our desires occur at random. However, as we saw above in the case of the fighter charmed by a succubus, compatibilist approaches don't work when we can see the causal mechanisms at play. As Max Planck (1858–1947), one of the founders of quantum physics, concluded, "The freedom of the human will has been put forward as offering logical grounds for the acceptance of only a statistical causality operative in the physical universe ... I do not at all agree with this attitude. If we should accept it, then the logical result would be to reduce the human will to an organ which would be subject to the sway of mere blind chance."[5] As long as our desires are not under our control, we aren't acting freely when we do as we desire. So whether our actions are caused by prior events or uncaused, we were not acting freely and are not to blame for them.

Four-Dimensional Dungeons and Powerless Dragons

If there is any lingering doubt in your mind as to whether anybody could ever be acting freely, whether they be devil, orc, or human being, one final consideration should put it to rest. Nobody can ever act freely because there is already a fact about how we are going to act over the entire course of our lives. For every second to come, there is already a fact about what you will be doing in that second, whether you will be working, or committing a crime, or running a wise and mystical druid on a quest for a ring that shoots fireballs.

We normally tend to think of the future as being open – to think that there are a variety of different ways that the future might turn out. This is contrasted with the past, which we think of as being closed – we think of the past as being "set" in a way that the future is not. We take it that there is a fact about whether you spent yesterday hacking your way through the halls of the fire giant chieftain, but not yet a fact about whether you will spend tomorrow arguing over the division of treasure from the run and whether the party sorcerer needs a set of magic bagpipes just as much as your bard does.

However, the only difference between what we call the future and what we call the past is where they are in time relative to *us*, whether they are located after us in time, "the future," or before us in time, "the past." We view yesterday – when you met the giants in combat and handed them their enormous asses – as "the past" because it is located earlier in time than the moment in which you read this sentence. We view tomorrow – when you shout and fling dice around the room in rage at the sorcerer's player – as "the future" because it is located later in time than the moment in which you read this sentence. However, Albert Einstein's (1879–1955) Special Theory of Relativity implies that no time is ever objectively "past," "present," or "future." On Einstein's model of the universe, whether two events are occurring at the same time depends on the frame of reference from which you are observing them. Because there is no objective fact about which things are happening at the same time, there can't be a time that is uniquely *present*. Likewise, there can be no objective *past* or *future*, since events are only ever past or future relative to *us*. It is tempting but wrong to think of the universe as a three-dimensional space moving forward in time as the future becomes the present, and the present becomes the past. In reality, the universe is four-dimensional space-time and the whole never moves or changes. What we call our "future" is every bit as set as the past, because from some frame of reference in the universe, what we call our future is already "the past." There is already a fact about whether you will have your bard try to kill the sorcerer tomorrow, just as much as there is a fact about whether you had your bard try to kill the sorcerer yesterday.

How does this relate to free will? Let's go back to our newly spawned glabrezu demon, fresh from the elemental chaos. For the glabrezu to have free will, there must be a sense in which it gets to control what it does in its life, a sense in which it is up to the demon how it acts. It must be able to choose whether it will give in to its wicked and anarchic instincts, roaming the planes in search of clerics to carve, fighters to fillet, and druids to disembowel, or whether it will turn its back on violence and destruction, and use its jagged claws to make bandages at a hospital for impoverished gnomes.

However, if we assume that space-time functions in the worlds of *D&D* in the same way that it functions in our universe, then at the moment the glabrezu is created there is already a fact of the matter about how it will spend the rest of its life. Indeed, there has *always* been a fact about how the glabrezu will live – there was a fact about it millions of years before the demon came into being. In what sense, then, can we insist that the glabrezu really has a choice about how to act, when it has always been a fact that it will, say, dedicate its existence to pinching the noses off paladins? Even if the glabrezu's will to perform involuntary cosmetic surgery on the best and bravest of good's soldiers will be a link in the causal chain leading from the demon's coalescence from fundamental forces of nature to an infamous career of nose-related violent crime, the fact that it was already true long before the demon existed that it would commit a string of nasal atrocities means that the demon never had any genuine say in the matter. The glabrezu *couldn't* have done otherwise, because the future was already *set*. Importantly, nothing about the future being set requires that events do not happen at *random*. Even if we rule that the elemental chaos is an entirely random system that spits out monsters who have the form they have for no prior reason at all, relativity implies that there will still be a *fact* about the sort of creatures that will be vomited forth and what cruel and riotous acts they will perform after they arrive.

What goes for fresh demons goes for everybody else – as the saying goes, what's good for the glabrezu is good for the grell.

Since the future is set, nobody has free will. The infant roper, newly hatched, can't truly have a choice about whether to be a killer if it is already a fact that in the next twenty years it will slaughter twenty dwarves, devouring their flesh and, for some reason known only to itself, storing their treasure in its "special gizzard." The same applies to those who turn to evil after having had every advantage in life. An evil human cleric of Bane, god of war and conquest, may have been raised by a loving family to be a devoted follower of the merciful Pelor, only to turn to Bane out of greed and a hunger for power. Yet the cleric is blameless because she never had a free choice in the matter – even when she was an innocent child, sincerely singing hymns of Pelor's light; it was already a fact that she would one day raze her home city with an army of goblins and put the whole population to the sword.

As for you and me, we experience the world as if we were free, but this is an illusion. Our conception of freedom requires that the future must be in some way open for us, but the future is not open to us because there are already facts about what we will do. Either it is a fact that you will play *D&D* tomorrow or it is a fact that you won't. Either way, your "choice" tomorrow is set. Either it is a fact that you will steal your friends' dice the next time you play or it is a fact that you won't. Either way, it isn't in any meaningful sense "up to you." Perhaps most importantly of all, what goes for demons and monsters and you and me goes for those who are labeled "evil" in this world. For every crime that has ever been committed, it has been a fact throughout time that that crime would be committed in just that way by just that person at just that moment. This means that no crime has ever genuinely been committed out of free will.

Free Will and Other Imaginary Monsters

Abandoning the myth of "free will" should lead us to change the way we think about wrongdoers. The notion of retributive justice – that is, just punishment – relies on the existence of free will. It cannot be just to punish someone for doing something that they couldn't help doing, as the falling cleric said to the spiteful rogue. Meting out suffering to make sure that people suffer as much as they deserve to makes no sense, because nobody deserves to suffer at all – not the pit fiend reigning in hell, not the drow making conquest deep underground, not the worst criminal on Earth. Our attention needs to be focused instead on reducing suffering for everyone. That doesn't mean that we must never make someone suffer for their crime, but the goal must always be the alleviation of suffering as a whole, never the infliction of suffering because suffering is *deserved*. Drawing the distinction between useful suffering and *deserved* suffering isn't just a matter of chopping hairs. It is, for instance, the difference between a humane and constructive prison system and an inhumane and destructive one.

At its most extreme, the deserved suffering model of justice might approve an institution like the Nine Hells from *D&D*. Indeed, as noted above, we *have* to assume that the justice of deserved suffering is what explains the lack of concern shown by the forces of good for conditions in hell. Bone devil taskmasters terrorize the bearded devil soldiers, ice devils twist the limbs off squealing imps just for being weak, and the chain devils gleefully skin alive anyone they can get their talons on. Meanwhile, the lesser damned are choking in the acid swamps of Minauros on level 3, being horribly burned in the firepits of Phlegethos on level 4, freezing their asses off on the Stygian tundra on level 5, or are otherwise in torment from the environment alone, all the while waiting for the moment when they are noticed by a higher-ranking citizen of hell and brutally tortured. Hell in *D&D* is a bad place for bad people to live in so that bad things can happen to them. Such an infernal institution could not be justified if we only ever inflict suffering to *reduce* suffering. Ripping someone apart with chains or biting them with a beard made of snakes not only hurts *them*, but it makes it less likely, rather than more likely, that they will be successfully rehabilitated. Making people suffer is one of the weakest tools we have for improving behavior, and one of the most counter-productive if over-applied.

It is too much to hope for that humans can give up on using the notion of "blame." It seems too tied to our emotional makeup for us to be able to abandon it on intellectual grounds. When the Greek philosopher Zeno of Citium (334–262 BCE) caught one of his slaves stealing, and the slave protested that according to Zeno's own theories he was destined the steal, Zeno simply answered, "Yes, and to be whipped for it too."[6] We humans, with our psychological need to see blameworthiness, are like boneclaws and wights, bound by their very nature to hate the living. There is nothing about being alive that makes someone deserving of hatred, but the wights just can't *see* things that way, just because of the way they are built.

However, that we are forced to experience the universe a certain way because of the sort of creature that we are does not prevent us from recognizing that our experiences are *misleading* and don't capture reality. A grell is blind, but the grell can still understand *that* it is blind; it can appreciate that there are things it isn't seeing. Just as relativity has shown that our experience of time as consisting in past, present, and future is illusionary, so it can be seen that human belief in free will likewise rests on a misunderstanding of physics. We cannot be free if our actions are caused and we cannot be free if our actions are uncaused, and we cannot be free because our future is every bit as set as our past. Thus, it would make sense for us to move away from a justice-based approach to dealing with crime to a utility-based approach that is concerned only with improving conditions for everyone.

Perhaps the next time you defeat a mind flayer, you will not just run it through with your longsword and use its tentacles for fishing bait, but will seek out a home for criminally insane cephalopods, somewhere that the mind flayer can live in the dark and dankness, expressing itself through disturbing paintings of subterranean cities and graphic scenes of brain-eating. Perhaps the next time you have the fiery immolith demon at your mercy, you will spare it extinguishment by *polar blast* and *greater ice storm* spells, and instead set it free on a deserted rocky island, to spend its days in harmless conflagration, incinerating small crabs and spiders and screaming *deathfire* curses at the clouds. Or perhaps not. *D&D* is a game, and games should be played in whatever way is most fun. If you have more fun turning mind flayers into calamari with a +3 longsword of mollusk slaying and dealing with immolith by flushing the dungeon with water spells, then more power and xp to you. The same goes if you have more fun slaughtering innocent halflings or tearing the wings off harmless pixies – whatever you like to *pretend* to do is just fine with me. It is what you do in *this* world that reveals your true alignment.

Notes

1. Wizard's RPG Team, *Monster Manual*, 4th edn. (Renton, WA: Wizards of the Coast, 2008), p. 7.
2. Titus Lucretius Carus, *On the Nature of the Universe*, trans. R.E. Latham (New York: Penguin Classics, 1994), p. 45.
3. Paul-Henri Thiry (Baron) d'Holbach, *The System of Nature*, vol. 1 (Seattle, WA: CreateSpace, 2011), p. 2.
4. Thomas Hobbes, *Leviathan*, ed. J.C.A. Gaskin (Oxford: Oxford University Press, 2009), p. 140.
5. Max Planck, *Where is Science Going?* (Woodbridge, CT: Ox Bow Press, 2004), p. 30.
6. Diogenes Laertius, *The Lives and Opinions of Eminent Philosophers*, trans. R.D. Hicks (Cambridge, MA: Harvard University Press, 1925), Book VII, p. 175.

Paragons and Knaves
Does Good Character Make for a Good Character?

J.K. Miles and Karington Hess

In R.A. Salvatore's enormously popular first novel in the Legend of Drizzt saga, *Homeland*, Zaknafein, the father of one of the most beloved characters in contemporary fantasy literature, Drizzt Do'Urden, denounces his drow heritage. In a soliloquy he recognizes that in the chaotic evil world of the drow, he is different. He laments the tragedy that he does not share the alignment of his kin. "Zaknafein Do'Urden, I am called, yet a Drow I am not, by choice or by deed." His moral character is not aligned with the treachery, violence, and cunning that permeates the Underdark kingdom. This same misalignment will prompt his son Drizzt to renounce his home and kin and begin his long trek to the surface world where he will become a virtuous hero.

There is plenty of room for debate in *Dungeons & Dragons* as to the importance alignment plays in character development. It should not be surprising, however, that as moral philosophers our contention is that alignment is more than just a way to determine one's character class. A character's alignment is the way that she ought to interact with the other players and the world created by the DM. In this chapter we aim to do the following:

Dungeons & Dragons and Philosophy: Read and Gain Advantage on All Wisdom Checks, First Edition. Edited by Christopher Robichaud.
© 2014 John Wiley & Sons, Inc. Published 2014 by John Wiley & Sons, Inc.

(1) Clarify why alignment is an important component in character creation and development.
(2) Demonstrate how applying moral philosophy and introducing ethical dilemmas that allow the players to make meaningful moral choices leads to a more rewarding gaming experience.
(3) Highlight how one of philosophy's most enduring and frustrating questions, "Why be good?" becomes salient whenever we are deciding what kind of character to make.

Good philosophy starts by defining its terms. But what is alignment in *D&D*? The short answer is that it is an element of the player's character sheet that clarifies their worldview and moral outlook. It is also a category that can limit character class and an aura that allows spells or abilities to detect a character's moral outlook – and if necessary "smite" that evil (or good) into oblivion. There is much more to say, of course, because wizards and philosophers rarely settle for the short and easy answer.

Let's start by examining the concept of alignment. To be aligned is to be fit with something. We talk of factions being aligned when their purposes fit. Unlike in our world, good and evil are active forces. Characters are aligned with these moral forces. Zaknafein's speech and Drizzt's exile from the Underdark are compelling because their moral outlook is at odds with treachery, scheming, and chaotic evil nature of the drow. In medieval society slavery, inequality, and torture were not only tolerated but institutionalized. The player-characters may not, depending on their alignment choice, be willing to tolerate these evils. Obviously the good, altruistic characters will have a more difficult time in this society than characters who are only self-interested.

The Good, the Bad, and the Legendary

The players fill the role of protagonists in the story. It is up to the DM to create the rest of the world – anything from the town drunk to the vile arch-lich. It is also up to the DM to foster character growth because this is what drives story. Character growth is not the same as leveling up. Getting to level 20 is not nearly as interesting as the naive but zealous paladin who swears death to all orcs, but who is forced to decide whether to slay innocent orc children who will likely grow up to plague the countryside. How players react to such difficult moral choices becomes the stuff of legend. As the *Book of Exalted Deeds* says, "Let their choices be difficult but not deadly ... Let their choices and actions matter." If this is true, your campaign can benefit from a little moral theory.

A few well-designed ethical dilemmas can encourage your characters to make some meaningful decisions. There should be no obviously right choice and their decision should have lasting effects in the world. Aragorn would just be a great ranger and would-be ruler without the temptation of the One Ring. Where his ancestors fail, Aragorn triumphs through a series of meaningful moral choices. Without the long trek from Menzoberranzan, Drizzt would just be a dark-skinned ranger with dual wielding. What makes both of these rangers special is that they make the hard choices. It is our hope that the characters in your campaign will also become the kind of legendary heroes that your players will reminisce about ten years after the last die roll. Of course, that's only true if DMs and players want a rich gaming session that is more than "Hack, Slash, and get the Shiny." (After all, if that's what you want, there's always Warhammer!)

Taking Alignment Seriously

D&D attracts imaginative players. Your party will likely be filled with virtuous paragons, nefarious knaves, and pragmatists. The right way to think about alignment has long been a controversy in *D&D*. This is not surprising given that morality is controversial in the real world. In the beginning of *Dungeons & Dragons* (original edition), there were three alignments – law, neutrality, and chaos. *Advanced Dungeons & Dragons'* alignment system added the axis of good/evil to form the canonical nine alignments. In the fourth edition the alignment system underwent its most drastic change since the addition of good and evil. Fourth edition alignment jettisoned four of the alignments and left only the following: lawful good, good, unaligned, evil, and chaotic evil. At the time of this writing, the authors have seen playtests of what is now called *D&D: Next*. The nine-point alignment system is back but its role has not been fully presented.

The role of alignment in character creation throughout, however, has always been ambiguous and left up to players and the DM to consider how much alignment matters to their role-playing. Some DMs go so far as to remove alignment from their campaign entirely. As long-time players and DMs, we understand that some parts of the gaming have to be left fluid. Gary Gygax, the All-Father of RPGs, once remarked that what must never be told to DMs is that they don't really need the rules. However, we think that the role of alignment in role-playing, like the contributions of Gygax himself, has never been given its due. After all, the second edition puts alignment choice at the end of the character creation process. In *3.5 Player's Handbook*, alignment is not covered until chapter 6 – after feats but before equipment.

As philosophers, we hope you will consider supplementing your game library with a little Aristotle, Kant, and Hume when designing your encounters. As fellow gamers we think alignment should be an important part of character and campaign development. Alignment may not be as constricting as the Iron Bands of Bilarro, but should be taken into account when a character faces a meaningful choice. It should not be an afterthought. Without the moral constraints, paladins are just self-righteous clerics with a better attack bonus and some nifty supernatural abilities.

With that in mind, let's look at the two major components in alignment (good/evil and law/chaos) and subject them to a little ethical analysis.

What we mean by "good," and by extension "evil," is a perennial question in philosophy. It may be *the* debate in moral philosophy. In the *D&D* source books there isn't a lot of debate. Good characters are distinguished by their concern for the well-being of others. Neutral characters show only self-concern, while evil characters tend to harm others or place others in harm's way for personal gain. Lawful characters tend to follow the rules given to them by society. Neutral characters follow the rules only when it is advantageous to them or they fear being caught. Chaotic characters actively seek to disrupt the rules placed on them by society, whether to promote social change or incite anarchy.

The Book of Vile Darkness suggests that if you take morality in this manner, "What is good?" is answered by using a spell or supernatural ability that detects a person's alignment, or whoever is affected by *holy smite*. Because good and evil are tangible forces, some creatures are intrinsically good and others evil. Demons and chromatic dragons are evil. Celestials and metallic dragons are good. Simple enough, but not very philosophical.

Can good people do evil things for good reasons and still remain good? What if we wanted our concept of good and evil to be more than merely forces? *The Book of Vile Darkness* suggests an interesting variant in which good and evil stem from the considered habits and practices of the character. *The Book of Exalted Deeds* expands upon this, "Being Good requires a certain temperament, the presence of virtues that spur a character, not just avoid evil or its appearance, but actively promote good." In other words, whether a paladin is good or evil is judged by his repeated actions. Doing virtuous actions creates virtuous character. Doing evil actions creates vicious character.

This is not something the Wizards of the Coast pulled out of a bag of holding. It was the reigning ethical theory for roughly 2,500 years. Virtue theory found it greatest proponents in Socrates, Plato, and Aristotle. Aristotle codified his moral theory in what we now call virtue ethics. One becomes virtuous not by taking a character class but by making choices that develop into habits that in turn form moral character. It seems to us that this variant provides a moral framework that is great for role-playing. Therefore, we will use this virtue-based variant as the "Tavern" from which we will launch our campaign into the philosophical Underdark.

For virtue ethicists, the moral question is not primarily "What is the right thing to do?" but "What kind of person do I want to be?" The second edition *Player's Handbook* says, "The character cannot wake up one morning and say, 'I think I'll become lawful good today.' (Well, he can say it, but it won't have any effect.)"[1]

So now that we have mapped out the territory a bit, let's focus on the ethical dilemmas that alignment is supposed to help us resolve. We'll discover that no matter how deep our understanding of alignment it isn't going to be the divination spell we need to make those character-defining choices.

Paladins and Trolleys

If ethical choices make a good campaign memorable, how then can moral theory help us make ethical choices? The stock and trade of moral theory is the thought experiment called the "Trolley Problem," first proposed by contemporary philosopher Philippa Foot, but made famous by Judith Jarvis Thomson. The Trolley Problem is a thought experiment designed to test our intuitions about what makes an action wrong. In its basic form the thought experiment asks us to imagine a trolley going down a set of tracks. Up ahead is a fork in the tracks. Stranded on the tracks is a busload of people, and without a track switch they will surely be killed. However, on the other track there is one innocent individual. Most people agree with the moral principle that, all things being equal, saving a busload of people is the right action to take even if it results in the loss of an innocent life. However, suppose saving the busload wasn't just a matter of flipping a switch but rather pushing someone in front of the train (assuming you couldn't sacrifice yourself). The outcome is exactly the same. Lots of people live and one person dies, but somehow it doesn't seem right to actively kill someone to save a busload of people.

Figure 2.1 shows an example of an upper-level encounter that incorporates a moral dilemma like the Trolley Problem. In the midst of a quest that will save hundreds of lives, our party, composed of three non-evil characters, has been ambushed and

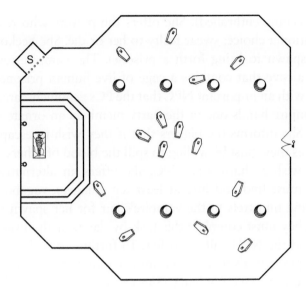

Figure 2.1

subdued. After many hours they awaken in a daze. They are weaponless, robbed of any magical items, and trapped in individually sealed coffins. Once they break free they find that they are in a dimly lit room. As their eyes adjust to the darkness they discover that they are in an enormous underground mausoleum with a large marble tomb effigy as the most prominent fixture in the room. Closer inspection reveals many more coffins are haphazardly scattered throughout the forbidding chamber. Opening any of the coffins requires a DC 15 strength check and reveals a slumbering vampire. Attempting to open the marble sepulcher requires a DC 25 strength check and reveals a beautiful female vampire who immediately awakens. Opening any of the coffins or the marble sepulcher will cause all the vampires to awaken in 1D8 rounds. The last to awaken is the master vampire, who emerges slowly and gracefully from her marble tomb if it was not disturbed previously.

The rest of the vampires begin to eye the party with a ravenous hunger, but do not attack. The master vampire slowly approaches the party and attempts to enthrall by using her dominate ability (as the spell *dominate person* (Su) (12th-level caster) will save DC

18 or become enthralled). She offers the players who resist her domination a choice: swear fealty to her or die. She beckons one of her spawn to bring forth a prisoner. The vampire reveals a hidden alcove that contains a cage of live human prisoners and returns with an important NPC that the PCs genuinely care about. The vampire hands one of the party members an ornate mithril dagger. She informs the players that if they wish to escape with their lives they must be willing to spill the blood of others. If they do not wish to harm this NPC, she offers an alternative. The players must find and lure at least ten villagers, vagabonds, or wandering minstrels to the vampire's lair for her spawn to consume. They must complete this task by dawn or the lives of the party and the NPC will be forfeit. To further complicate things, the vampire reveals that she has information that is critical to the players' quest. She is not lying. (She actually does have such useful information and will give it to the characters when they have either killed the innocent or brought victims back to the lair.) The master vampire is no stranger to deception and will send a few of her "children" to observe their progress. If there is any hint of deception they will attack.

Alignment doesn't solve this problem, because alignment only tells us what's permissible, not what is obligatory. Good characters should not kill innocent NPCs, but what other choice do they have? They could heroically sacrifice their lives, taking as many vampires as they can before they die. Of course if they do that, their previous task will be left unfinished and hundreds will suffer the consequences.

Is it consistent with good alignment to sacrifice one innocent to save hundreds? *The Book of Exalted Deeds* says such trade-offs are inconsistent with good alignment. Philosophy, however, has been considering these dilemmas since long before the *D&D* box set ever hit store shelves.

For instance, utilitarians would say the right thing to do is what would produce the greatest amount of pleasure and the least amount of suffering for everyone. The moral choice is simply a matter of addition and subtraction. Let's say the lawful neutral mage, an illusionist, is a consummate utilitarian. A quick calculation says the loss of one life is regrettable but necessary to save hundreds. And besides, she points out to the paladin, there's always the *atonement* spell. Now suppose the paladin is a deontologist. For deontologists, lives simply can't be weighed like so much loot. To do so would be to treat someone as merely a means to some outcome no matter how good. If our paladin had read his Immanuel Kant (1724–1804), he would believe he cannot lie. Lying to the vampire uses her as merely a means to an end and fails to respect her as a rational agent.

You can imagine the moral debate. But we're not done. Suppose the neutral good cleric of Pelor chimes in that they are both mistaken. Virtue ethics isn't about calculations or an absolute universal law against anything. Rather, it's about character. He thinks lying in order to escape isn't corrupting because it's not something any of the party does on a regular basis. He may suggest that if the Paladin can't lie, it doesn't mean the character with the highest bluff skill can't make a false promise until they can fight this battle on better terms. In other words, alignment gives us constraints; virtue ethics gives us choices.

All of this debate might prompt a player to say "By all the nine hells, why would I want to play a character with a good alignment?" In other words, in *D&D* doesn't the vampire encounter above prove "Good guys finish dead" or "broken-hearted" or both? This too, it's not surprising, is a question that a little philosophical reflection can make … more complicated.

The Ring of Gyges and the Arch-Lich

For men are good in but one way, but bad in many. Excellence then is a state concerned with choice … being determined by reason.

—Aristotle

'Tis not contrary to reason to prefer the destruction of the whole world to the scratching of my finger.

—David Hume

Why would a player want to be a good-aligned character? This is a variation of a much older question in philosophy: Why be good at all? It was first asked by a character in Plato's *Republic*. Playing devil's advocate, the character Glaucon thinks that if there was a way that we could escape punishment, it wouldn't be irrational to be evil. He tells a tale of a magic ring that would make the wearer invisible. If the ring gave ultimate power without any consequences no one would choose to be virtuous. The rest of the *Republic* is designed show why being good is the rational thing to do. Ultimately Plato says it makes sense to be good because a good person is one who balances their reason, passion, and appetites. Only those who cultivating virtue are truly at peace.

Aristotle (384–322 BCE) goes further, arguing that it isn't rational to be like the lawful good but neither is it rational to just be evil. The way of virtue is a middle ground between extremes. If goodness required too much sacrifice at the expense of one's own life, that kind of good is irrational, but so is a life totally devoted to being self-consumed. Essentially Aristotle makes the argument that everyone ought to strive to realize their full potential. For all humans (and elves, orcs, etc.) that potential is to be rational creatures. And rational creatures pursue virtue in a balanced way.

If Aristotle were to look over your shoulder when you were deciding alignment, he wouldn't necessarily advise choosing lawful good since it might entail too much sacrifice. He would not, however advocate resorting to evil alignments since playing at vice is irrational.

Some might argue that Aristotle wouldn't object to playing an evil character. The closest Aristotle comes to discussing role-playing is in his *Poetics*, where he considers whether or not it is good to identify with a villainous character in a Greek tragedy. This identification can lead to a kind of catharsis where we are purged of our own evil desires. So could role-playing an evil character have the same effect? It is unlikely because the only way that we can be purged is if the villains we identify with arouse in us both pity and fear.

Suppose your epic-level character has the choice to become an arch-lich. Should you agree to trade your goodness for ultimate power? As most us know, arch-liches are some of the most powerful villains in the *D&D* multiverse. They can hold their own with archons and demon lords. They have no fear of death since if they are destroyed they re-spawn in 1D10 days unless someone destroys their hidden phylactery. While drow are born into treachery and vampires may have been turned against their will, liches *choose* to forsake goodness for power.

Aristotle would question the rationality of playing a lich. Acting out that kind of evil and vice with little consideration for arousing pity and fear is not going enhance the player's own moral character.

But suppose we introduce another philosopher, David Hume (1711–76), who totally disagrees with Aristotle that it's irrational to be evil. Hume thinks being good or evil has nothing to do with being rational or irrational. Hume says, a knave can be both perfectly sensible and wholly evil like an arch-lich. However, Hume would probably agree with Aristotle that you shouldn't play an arch-lich.

For Hume, morality is about sentiment, not reason. This is not a "gut feeling" as much as it is a kind of moral skill. Human beings are hard-wired to approve of certain virtues and to disapprove of certain vices. Moral evaluation is more like a skill check. One can put ranks in the skill by cultivating and examining the feelings of approval and disapproval that we experience when we see people engage in actions that can be considered moral or immoral. Just as someone who has a good appraise check can determine the value of a magical item accurately, a paragon of virtue can determine what the right thing to do is in difficult situations. This moral sense is tied to sympathy. A disinterested appreciation for human beings causes us to care for their well-being. Being so much more powerful than the average humanoid would dull the sense of sympathy, because an arch-lich has no fear of death, no concern for others, and no peers. Even though, there is nothing irrational about arch-lichdom, there is still something deeply immoral about it. In fact, both Aristotle and

Hume might well agree that if the player across the table from you wanted to play an arch-lich for an extended campaign, that choice speaks volumes about their moral character and might make you think twice about gaming with them.

Having now trekked through the philosophical underdark, we emerge into the warm light of day a bit dazzled but with an appreciation of alignment as both an important tool for gaming and moral reflection. Having subjected alignment to a little philosophical scrutiny, we hope that you have seen how alignment can enhance your gaming experience, and we hope that you can now bring some philosophy to the table the next time you fill out your character sheet.

Note

1. David "Zeb" Cook, *Advanced Dungeons & Dragons Player's Handbook*, 2nd edn. (Lake Geneva, WI: Tactical Studies Rules, 1995), p. 69.

Is Anyone Actually Chaotic Evil?

A Playable Theory of Willful Wrongdoing

Neil Mussett

My very first serious ethical debate was over a game of *D&D*. "I am going to switch to GURPS [Generic Universal Role Playing System]", my friend Joe told me, "because character creation makes much more sense. It doesn't have alignments, which is great. I mean, who really is 'chaotic evil'?" I tried to argue that we sometimes do what we know is wrong, but he was the DM, and he didn't listen (you know how they are).

As it turns out, accounting for the mechanics of willful wrongdoing has been a major problem for ethics from the beginning, and it has led to some very strange theories. Socrates and Plato simply deny the possibility. Aristotle tries to disagree with Plato, but fails in the end. Thomas Aquinas proposes a kind of genetic moral defect, but does not get much farther than Aristotle. Kant gives an account that even he admits is inconceivable. Dietrich von Hildebrand uses exotic metaphysical values and two scales of goodness. Hannah Arendt suggests that the majority of evil in the world is done out of stupidity.

Dungeons & Dragons and Philosophy: Read and Gain Advantage on All Wisdom Checks, First Edition. Edited by Christopher Robichaud.
© 2014 John Wiley & Sons, Inc. Published 2014 by John Wiley & Sons, Inc.

While all these theories may be very interesting to the philosopher, the average *D&D* player only needs to know one thing: How do I play evil? If we evaluate these theories according to their *playability*, we can piece together a picture of the evil choice using the most game-friendly points of each theory.

No Dice

Like good Dungeon Masters, we have to set some ground rules before we go. First: no denying free will. Richard Dawkins (chaotic neutral), the atheist/biologist, believes that although we *feel* free, our physical makeup actually determines our actions:

> Even if you are in some sense a determinist … that doesn't mean we have to behave as if we are determinists, because the world is so complicated, and especially human brains are so complicated, that we behave as if we are not deterministic, and we feel as if we are not deterministic – and that's all that matters.[1]

Dawkins may be right, and we may not be free, but that effectively reduces us all to non-player-characters, which won't do. No choice, no evil.

On the other hand, there can be no evil without morality. The English philosopher J.L. Mackie (1917–81, neutral) thinks that even though most people believe there really is such a thing as good and evil, they're dead wrong:

> Although most people in making moral judgments implicitly claim, among other things, to be pointing to something objectively prescriptive, these claims are all false.[2]

He has some wonderful arguments for what he calls moral subjectivism, attempting to show that all moral judgments are ultimately nothing more than expressions of personal preference. However, if there is no real difference between right and wrong, there can be no good or evil characters. Asmodeus might as well be a unicorn; gold and red dragons just have different styles. No standard, no evil.

Finally, no consequentialism. This is a bit more technical, but think for a minute about how the utilitarian John Stuart Mill (1806–73, lawful neutral) describes morality:

> The motive has nothing to do with the morality of the action, though much with the worth of the agent. He who saves a fellow creature from drowning does what is morally right, whether his motive be duty, or the hope of being paid for his trouble; he who betrays the friend that trusts him, is guilty of a crime, even if his object be to serve another friend to whom he is under greater obligations.[3]

In other words, it does not matter why you made the choice; if your action made the world a happier place, it was a good action. If the opposite, then it was bad. Actually, the normal person doesn't even have to think about the world's happiness. Mill thinks it best for you to just take care of yourself and your friends.

Why is this a problem? It sounds realistic and comfortable, and it lets you take care of business: the show *24* might as well have been written by Mill. It is a problem because there is no way to *play* an evil utilitarian. Good and bad come from the effects of your actions, not your intentions. Sure, there might be some actions that tend to make everyone miserable, and you can try to do those as much as possible, but the DM decides what actually happens in the game. You might be such a pain that previously warring factions of elves unite to defeat you – which is ultimately a very good thing – which defeats the point of being evil.

Socrates, the First DM

Now that we have our rules set, we can introduce our characters. Who hasn't heard of Socrates (469–399 BCE, chaotic good)? You may know him from *Bill and Ted's Excellent Adventure*, and you may know that he had some sort of method, but it is easy to forget the details. He would have made a good DM: he spent most of his time in rowdy groups of young guys, asking them questions about magic rings, dungeon escapes, complicated mythical cities, and non-material worlds. One of his fans was a young man named Aristocles (nicknamed Plato by his wrestling coach). Plato (c.429–c.347 BCE, lawful neutral) had parents who wanted him to be a lawyer, but he had plans to be a poet. When he met Socrates, he decided to combine the two by writing mini-plays about Socrates and his arguments with tutors, politicians, and other assorted Greek big-wigs. Socrates never actually wrote anything; everything we have is from Plato.

Socrates was primarily interested in ethics at a time when other philosophers were interested in cosmology, chemistry, and physics. He gave us the famous line, "The unexamined life is not worth living."[4] Interestingly, Socrates didn't base his ethics on religion or societal norms, but on calculated self-interest. Suppose you decided to live your life pursuing every pleasure you could. You did your best to satisfy every one of your urges. In the process, your urges would become stronger; you would spend more time trying to fulfill them, and less time feeling full. Socrates compares this to a man who tries to keep a room full of leaky jars full:

> his vessels are leaky and decayed, and he is compelled to fill them constantly, all night and day, or else suffer extreme distress.[5]

Is this a happy life? We would use the word *addict* to describe the same thing, and it leads to "interminable trouble – leading the life of a robber."[6] It's actually more trouble to be bad than good. It's easier to live an orderly life, restraining your desires, because you'll be more easily satisfied. You won't have to work as hard at satisfying yourself, and you won't live a foul life, producing pain and harm in those around you.

It seems obvious to say that we want to be happy. We want "wisdom and health and wealth and everything else of that kind."[7] We go to work, we study, we pay our bills, we do all sorts of things that only make sense because they lead us closer to our vision of happiness. Socrates refers to this as "*the* good." It is our ultimate motivation:

everything we do should be for the sake of what is good ... [T]he good is the end of all our actions, and it is for its sake that all other things should be done, and not it for theirs.[8]

Evil, the opposite of good, is unhappiness. So why choose it? Why would you do something that you know will make you miserable? Maybe you were carried away; your desires were just too strong. You wanted food or sex or armor so much that you indulged your desires until you were left in poverty, disgrace, and disease. You recognized your actions as evil, yet you freely committed them because you were led on and distracted by the pleasure they produced.

Socrates rejects this argument because it rests on a confusion: pleasure is just a weak form of good (happiness), and pain a weak form of evil (misery). Saying that I chose evil because I was overcome with pleasure is the same as saying that I chose evil because I was overcome with good, which Socrates considers laughable. No, choosing evil amounts to getting a bad deal, to losing on the cost/benefit scale, or as Socrates puts it, "getting the greater evil in exchange for the lesser good."[9]

Here's the problem: you really *can't* knowingly choose evil under these conditions. If I see that, all things considered, choice A will make me happier than choice B, there is no way for me to choose B. If I did choose B, it must have been because I did not *know* A would have made me happier. You can try to raise all sorts of objections about masochists and irrational impulses, but in the end you can only explain a choice in terms of what was attractive to the chooser. If you chose something bad, it was because you didn't know it would make you unhappy. Knowing what will make you happy is therefore the key to the good life. This is what Socrates meant by his motto, "virtue is either wholly or partly wisdom."[10]

No one who either knows or believes that something else, which is in his power to do, is better than what he is doing, subsequently does the other, when he can do what is better.[11]

No evil. Just stupidity. As you can imagine, that caused some controversy.

What does this mean for *D&D*? First of all, it means that nobody chooses evil *for the sake of evil*, what some people call diabolic evil. My friend Mike, when he taught me to play, told me that being chaotic evil meant that if I see a frog on a log, the frog will be dead after I pass it. However, this does not quite make sense; there is nothing in it for me. I have to connect it to my own happiness, to something I want for its own sake. Yes, I may attack strangers, but it is because I want to keep them off my land so that I can dig for gold, or I want to build my own reputation so I can gain power. I may be "chaotic" in that I don't want to establish some sort of army or have henchmen, but it will never be completely divorced from my vision of the good life.

If we are going to be pure Platonists, that means that our character will never act against our own happiness if we can help it. The evil character is deluded about life and how it all goes together, and so systematically chooses unhappiness. Not bad, just misguided.

Is this really the most playable theory? We've got 2,300 years of ethics; can't we do better?

Aristotle – Unearthed Arcana

I was one of those geeky DMs who stayed up late at night reading *Unearthed Arcana* and *Dragon Magazine*, looking for material to incorporate into my worlds. I imagine that Aristotle (384–322 BCE, lawful neutral) would have been much the same. Just as Plato was Socrates' best student, Aristotle was Plato's. Like Plato, he wrote dialogues, but unlike Plato, we don't have a single copy. For the most part, we only have his students' notes to represent his philosophy. They are a bit dry – I have heard them described as resembling VCR manuals – but what they lack in dramatic flair, they make up for in content. Aristotle covered all the bases – ethics, politics, drama, biology, physics, logic, you name it.

Like Socrates and Plato, he believed that ethics is about happiness:

> Now such a thing happiness, above all else, is held to be; for this we choose always for self and never for the sake of something else.[12]

So far, so good, but isn't this just a platitude? What does happiness mean anyway? Aristotle wants to give a meatier definition. The happy life is the good life, and when we talk about anything good, we are talking about meeting some sort of standard. A good DM is someone who has a good story ready when we show up and doesn't drive us crazy looking up rules. A good player is someone who stays in character and doesn't hog the barbecue chips and Jolt. Being good means living up to your unique role. It means exhibiting the appropriate excellence, or virtue.

What is unique about mankind? The closest thing to us is the higher animals, who have everything we do except for our minds. We have a special kind of rationality, and we can organize our lives accordingly. As humans, our highest virtue is to live the rational life in the society of other people. Other virtues flow from this, like courage, generosity, and honesty. We can obtain these virtues through habit, by repeatedly performing courageous acts, for example. Possessing these virtues is something pleasurable – a generous person enjoys giving, for instance. A happy life, of course, is pleasurable, but it is something more: it is fulfilling all of your potential. We even use a special word for Aristotle's brand of happiness: *eudaemonia*.

What about evil? By all accounts, Aristotle was more grounded in the real world than Plato. He developed much of his philosophy through observation of the world around him. He knew about politics, and he knew that some people are very wicked.

He didn't like Socrates' theory of wrongdoing. Socrates said that you only choose the bad because of ignorance. But this does not jibe with our experience. I did not hit you over the head with a bottle because I thought I it was the right thing to do. We know first-hand that there are times we act against our best judgment (which he calls being incontinent[13]).

Aristotle gives a shot at various ways out of Socrates' position: Maybe I didn't really know it was wrong. Maybe that was just my opinion, and when it came down to it, my appetites were just too strong for anything but certainty. I knew that getting my hands on your vorpal sword would make me really, really happy, but I only suspected that there was something wrong in feeding you to a gelatinous cube.

Aristotle doesn't buy this one. If it were just a simple judgment call, a case of a strong conviction beating a weak one, people would sympathize with me. As it is, "we do not sympathize with wickedness, nor with any of the other blameworthy states."[14] It is not the sort of thing the virtuous man would do.

Maybe having a strong desire is like being drunk, or crazy, or asleep. I know that it's wrong, but my gold lust temporarily blinds me to my knowledge of the fact that I shouldn't rob members of my party. Aristotle reminds us that "outbursts of anger and sexual appetites and some other such passions ... actually alter our bodily condition, and in some men even produce fits of madness."[15] In that state, you could still talk about right and wrong if someone asked you to, but it would be like the "utterance by actors on the stage"; you wouldn't connect the universal rule to your particular circumstances.

Aristotle likes this answer, but it presents a problem. A big problem. The problem is that it really isn't any different than Socrates' answer. He admits as much:

> the position that Socrates sought to establish actually seems to result; for it is not in the presence of what is thought to be knowledge proper that the affection of incontinence arises (nor is it this that is "dragged about" as a result of the state of passion), but in that of perceptual knowledge.[16]

You don't choose what you know is evil, because the only way to choose it is to be driven so mad with desire that you forget that it is wrong. Aristotle sounds depressed at the end of the chapter:

This must suffice as our answer to the question of action with and without knowledge, and how it is possible to behave incontinently with knowledge.[17]

Is there anything we can use from Aristotle's philosophy beyond what we got out of Socrates and Plato? Yes: the concepts of virtue and vice are supremely useful. When you have a virtue, you enjoy exercising it. If you are courageous, you enjoy being brave. If you aren't an honest person, you may be honest in this or that situation, but it will be more difficult for you, and you won't get a warm, fuzzy feeling when you do it. It would be interesting to have a character who is brave and honest, but not generous or forgiving.

It is also important to keep in mind that you act differently depending on your state of mind. Aristotle distinguishes between impulsive and deliberate actions, between voluntary and involuntary actions, by what is going on inside your head and heart. Your choices depend on your knowledge, your experience, your emotional state, and your long-term habits. An elf who is in the habit of keeping her cool will be able to avoid distractions, but a berserker may sabotage his own plan by losing his temper at the wrong moment. You can't play your character as a mere game piece – only the perfect person makes completely rational choices.

Thomas Aquinas – 15th-Level Cleric

You knew we had to have one, so here he is: the lawful good philosopher. St. Thomas Aquinas (1225–74) is our only philosopher who was born in a castle and carried a sword (at least while he was young). Armed with relics, he wandered a medieval world with a ragtag band of adventurers, gaining experience, and getting into (intellectual) fights. Like Plato, he grew up rich and well connected, and like Plato, he disappointed his parents by rejecting their wish that he go into politics. His father actually locked him in a tower to keep him from joining the begging friars, but his Mom arranged his escape and he became a cleric.

In Thomas' time, most Western philosophers followed Plato. It was only recently that scrolls of Aristotle were available to the Christian world (they had been preserved by Arabic philosophers). Thomas's teacher, St. Albert the Great (c.1193–1280, lawful good), was a famous scientist, and Thomas himself was more attracted to Aristotle's grounded, sense-based approach to the world than Plato's dreamy idealism.

Thomas was part of the Christian tradition, which had a heightened sense of the role of *choice* in good and evil. For Christians, there is one deity who is the embodiment of goodness. There is also a supremely evil being, who actually makes it into the *Monster Manual* under a few different names, and was once the most perfect creature, until he chose to reject God and led an army of fallen angels in a rebellion. A relatively junior angel named Michael led the army against him, and succeeded in expelling him from Heaven. He was then imprisoned in another location that appears surprisingly often in *D&D* modules. We live in a post-rebellion (aka fallen) world, where our choices in life determine which, *ahem*, plane will be our home for eternity.

Thomas sounds just like Aristotle in his definition of happiness:

> Now, the ultimate end of man, and of every intellectual sub-
> stance, is called felicity or happiness, because this is what every
> intellectual substance desires as an ultimate end, and for its own
> sake alone.[18]

However, Thomas takes a few steps beyond what he got from Aristotle. If we agree that happiness is living up to our fullest potential and the perfection of our powers, we also have to consider the fact that we are never completely happy in this life. There is no limit to our wants; we are never completely fulfilled. God is the one who gave us our desires and abilities, and God is the only one who can fulfill them. The things that will make us happy also happen to be the things that will draw us closer to God. We don't have to know this (most of us don't), because they have that effect on us whether we know it or not.

What is evil? Thomas defines evil as a privation. A privation is when something should have some sort of perfection, but it doesn't. Good examples of evil for Thomas include an iPod with no battery, or a backpack with no twenty-sided dice, or decaf anything. It is always a loss, a defect. There are different kinds: natural evil (toothaches, sauerkraut) and spiritual evil (murder, rape). We can put up with some natural evils like having our diseased arm cut off if it is going to give us something better, like not dying. The problem with spiritual evil is that what is lost is closeness with God, who is the only source of long-term happiness.

Thomas loved the writings of St. Augustine (354–430, chaotic good), who wrote a great deal about the effects of original sin. According to Augustine, "the deliberate sin of the first man is the cause of original sin."[19] We were never supposed to die or be miserable. The first man, Adam, was punished with death when he disobeyed God. This punishment was passed down to us, his children, much like a hereditary disease. We also inherit a predisposition to act like our first parents and do what we know to be wrong when it will get us something we really want. We commit our own personal sins because of the effects of the original sin.

Original sin opens the door to willful wrongdoing. Like Socrates, Plato, and Aristotle, Thomas agrees that we are only motivated by the good, which is tied to happiness. Like Aristotle, he talks about passions clouding our minds and making it more difficult to choose the good, but he also believes that we can act with certain malice, to "sin deliberately, as if one chooses what is bad knowingly."[20] Our insides are out of order, so to speak. I can choose the bad deal, ignoring the fact that it is going to burn me in the end. There are two main reasons I do it: first, it may be a weakness in my personality due to temperament or education, so an angry dwarf is more likely to get into fights he can't win, and a halfling raised in a thieves' guild will cheat at cards. Second, I may find myself in a situation where the normal obstacles to evildoing (e.g., punishment, castle walls) are lifted, and I can't control myself.

Once we commit evil, we make a habit, which makes it easier to become evil, because:

> to anyone that has a habit, whatever is befitting to him in respect of that habit, has the aspect of something lovable, since it thereby becomes, in a way, connatural to him, according as custom and habit are a second nature.[21]

In other words, once you steal that pack of Chewy Spree from the convenience store, the next one is much easier. Do it enough, and it's fun. An evil person is just a person in the habit of doing evil.

Thomas won't go as far as saying that you can completely rewire your sense of right and wrong, however. Virtue is a habit, too, and any time you do something good, you weaken your malice. Also, you can't change the natural consequences of your actions (that mob with pitchforks might cause you to reconsider your leadership style).

How does this help the game? First of all, we have the idea of fallen creatures. Men are fallen, meaning that they start out basically good, but with a certain limited vulnerability to doing evil. Unless you were raised in Mordor, you can only become an evil character with practice, and that has to be included in your backstory. Dwarves and halflings seem to have the same weakness. My sense from reading Tolkien is that he saw elves as un-fallen, which means that something awful and unnatural has to happen to an elf to make it evil (I never quite got the drow thing).

Secondly, Thomas introduces a notion of malice that is simply not there for the Greeks. Obviously, they understood what wicked people could do, but when they got around to describing it, it sounded like just a bit of stupid selfishness. Thomas tries to introduce a stronger sense of evil, and it worked – Dante's *Inferno* was based on Thomas's philosophy.[22]

Because he was so closely tied to Aristotle, however, there are those who don't think Thomas was able to get away from Socrates' original problem. If I can't help but want to be happy, and I see that a choice is not ordered to the good, then how can I choose it unless I am blinded by passion (and therefore not responsible)?

Monster Immanuel

Immanuel Kant (1724–1804, lawful neutral) was a German philosopher whose habits were so regular that people literally set their clocks by his daily walk. He was … tidy in his approach to philosophy. He would be the player who not only knows every rule in every edition of the game, but would be deeply upset about any conflicts (no matter how obscure). Although he was mild-mannered, he turned things completely upside down in several areas of philosophy, including ethics.

Kant gets a lot of flak for being a terrible writer, but you have to admire this:

> If a man who delights in annoying and vexing peaceable people at last receives a right good beating, this is no doubt a bad thing; but everyone approves it and regards it as a good thing, even though nothing else resulted from it.[23]

In other words, some guys need to get their butt kicked.

I say this half-joking, but think about what it means to say that it is a good thing for him to get pounded, "even though nothing resulted from it." The Greeks try to argue for morality based on happiness. That is very appealing, because they don't need to introduce God or rules or anything outside myself to make me want to be good. However, it does take away the notion of *deserving*. Socrates would say that getting knocked down would be a type of healing for this yahoo, but without the healing effects, punishment is simply pain, which is bad.

Kant disagrees. Unlike our first three philosophers, Kant is not a eudaemonist. Nowadays, his brand of ethics is called deontology, which is a combination of the Greek words for duty and logic. It takes a very different approach, with a very different starting point: "The only thing that is good without qualification or restriction is a good will."[24] Being smart is good, right? Depends on the person. Smart Gandalf? Good. Smart Morgoth? Bad. Just like in *D&D*, Kant believes that our attributes are independent of our alignment. Health, wealth, comeliness, wit, hairstyle, and even happiness itself can be bad if the person who has them is a lunatic serial puppy murderer. Good intentions are always good, and do not need anything else to make them good. Moral good and evil are about *motives*. My intentions are what make the difference.

You have to be good. This is a special kind of "have to," different than the same words in the sentence, "You have to use a tiny ball of bat guano and sulfur in order to cast the *fireball* spell." In the sentence, what is necessary is that you do X (use the bat poop) in order to do Y (cast the spell). Strictly speaking, do you have to use the poop? No. However, if you want to burn a path through those kobolds, then you do. Kant calls this a hypothetical imperative because of the whole if … then thing.

We don't experience morality as an if … then issue. "If you want to make friends, then you should not set fire to widows' houses." Or, "Since you want to stay out of jail, you should not murder that shopkeeper." Or even, "You want to be happy, so you must not sell your mother into slavery." Kant believes that we experience these as unconditional, absolute, "categorical" imperatives, which would be better phrased using the stronger "Thou shalt not …" formula.

Morality comes to us as a *law*, universally valid for all people. Kant calls this law a "a fact of reason" and "undeniable."[25] What is the law? It is close to the Golden Rule: do to others what you would be willing to have them do to you. Act using principles that you would be willing to turn into laws for everybody. Don't use or exploit people; treat them as an "end in themselves." If you do something hoping that other people won't follow your example, it is a bad thing.

The principle of your action, what Kant calls the maxim, is what is important, not the details. In other words, I do not have to hope that everybody moves to Buffalo and eats at this particular Ted's Hot Dogs. I do have to want everyone to follow my restaurant etiquette (e.g., don't cut in line, don't steal other people's Loganberry drinks, don't squirt ketchup on the elderly couple in the next booth).

OK, so if we accept Kant's claim that we have to be good, how on Earth (or The Outlands if you use those rules) can we be evil? Kant gives three main sources:

(1) *Weakness.* Even though the moral law is firm and unbending, I am not. I can see that I should do the right thing, but my inclinations point me elsewhere. Human nature is frail (halfling nature, too – think of Frodo in Mount Doom), and so we do not live up to our duties. This isn't exactly what we would call evil, but it is usually where evil gets its start.

(2) *Impurity.* From the outside, I may look like a Really Good Guy, helping a 1st-level wizard get experience, but I am only doing it to make her a more interesting target than myself. What's wrong with this? I do good things, but only for some sort of reward. Kant even goes so far as to say that it is a form of impurity to live a good life so that I can be happy. For Kant, the only good motive is duty for duty's sake. Unlike Aristotle and Aquinas, who say that virtue brings pleasure, Kant actually says that the best way to tell you are fulfilling your duty is if it hurts to do so.[26]

(3) *Depravity.* This is what we've been waiting for – corruption and perversity. Instead of living for duty, we can choose to live lives of ambition, or self-love, or other maxims. I want to become an epic-level fighter, and so everything I do is organized to get me the most experience possible. I care about this kingdom only to the extent that it allows me to sharpen my skills. Every so often, I may accidentally do something good, but because my attitude is "corrupted at its root,"[27] I am *evil*.

Who is evil for Kant? Everybody. Experience tells us that human nature has a universal propensity to deviate from the moral law. Aquinas calls this original sin and Socrates calls it weakness of will. Even the best of us has it; it is "woven into human nature."[28] This does not mean that we can choose evil for its own sake; Like the eudaemonists, Kant believes that "*Considered in themselves* natural inclinations are *good*."[29] However, we can choose to satisfy them at the expense of our duties.

If evil is universal, are we still to blame? Yes. If we are talking about how we choose, what sense does it make to say that something else caused it? Either it is a choice or it is not. Nothing is evil except for our own deeds. We can choose how to act, and we can choose the maxims that guide our actions. If I incorporate the (occasional) deviation from the moral law into my maxim, then I am evil, and nothing else is to blame.

So, how can we play-test this one? There is no denying that Kant is a bit on the complicated side. There is a lot more jargon to learn, and I don't envy the DM who tries to incorporate Kantian ethics into his rules. However, there is some interesting material to take away from his analysis: unlike our other philosophers, Kant places good and evil in the motivation of the character. Motivation will naturally lead a bad character to do bad things (and vice versa), but evil is there even before the bad effect. This changes evil into something more than bad judgment and self-destructive choices. There is an edge to evil in Kant that does not seem to be there for the first three.

His threefold scheme of weakness, impurity, and depravity give us a nice framework for character development. There can be different kinds of evil characters, and characters can advance from lesser to greater evil.

The "maxim" thing can actually be helpful. Each character has one maxim that guides his or her actions. Whatever does not fit in with the character's maxim is sacrificed, unless weakness comes into play. A purely good character will identify his or her duty and sacrifice everything (health, safety, experience, wealth) to live up to it. Evil characters will choose some other ambition (happiness, wealth, friendship) and sacrifice everything else, including duty, to fulfill that. Choosing a maxim is so important that it should be on page 1 of the character sheet.

As you can imagine, Kant's ethics is controversial. The authority of the moral law is obvious; doing good should be painful; everyone is evil; our inclination to evil is our fault: these claims are difficult to accept. Is there another approach using the same basic tools?

Dietrich von Hildebrand – Third Edition Rules

If there is one absolutely inescapable cliché in ethics, it is Adolf Hitler (1889–1945, lawful evil). For obvious reasons, Hitler is used as the ultimate example of human evil. Believe it or not, Hitler's ambassador to Austria believed that one of "the worst and most dangerous enemies of the Third Reich in Austria" was a philosopher. The ambassador informed Hitler that "the moving spirit behind these [anti-Nazi] machinations is the well-known emigrant, Professor Dietrich von Hildebrand."[30] Von Hildebrand ran an underground printing press, distributing an anti-Nazi newsletter in Austria. Hitler ordered him killed, but friends smuggled him to the United States, where he taught at Fordham University.

Compared to our other philosophers, von Hildebrand (1889–1977, lawful good) is relatively obscure. However, he got a pretty good first-hand look at evil, and it gave him quite a bit to say.

For von Hildebrand, ethics is about motivation. Not just anything can motivate us:

> Were we to ask a despairing man the reason for his sorrow, and were he to answer, "Because two and two are four," … We would suppose either he is putting us off for some reason, in refusing to tell us the true object of his sorrow, or else that he superstitiously connects these facts with some evil.[31]

Most of the facts around us are completely neutral. They have nothing that can move us, motivate us to act, or make us feel joy, sorrow, hope, or fear. Von Hildebrand would say that there is nothing important about them. Some things, like the location of a drinking fountain, may normally be neutral, but become important to me when I have just finished an ARMA workout.

Importance comes in two flavors: good and bad. Rabid dogs are as important as Christmas morning, but with a different character. The first repels me, inspires fear, and motivates me to high-tail it to the nearest lockable door. The second attracts me, inspires hope, and motivates me to procrastinate on sending out cards to my friends and family. Negative importance is what we call bad and vice versa.

The real key to von Hildebrand is what he calls the categories of importance.[32] There is not just one type of good and bad. On one hand, you have simple pleasure and pain, which is important only because of its connection with the things I like and don't like to experience. Next, you have things that are really good (or bad) for me, regardless of how I feel about them. A root canal is bad in the first sense because it is not subjectively satisfying, but good in the second because it is an objective good for me.

Then we think of Mom. I would like to call my mother good, but in what sense? She is not neutral, like the drying rack. If I call her good in the first sense, I am saying that she is only good to the extent that she puts me in a good mood. Take that away and she becomes as neutral as the color grey of the sidewalk. If I call her good in the second sense, I am really only saying that it is good for me to have a mother. Like hydration and daily vitamins, she is only important because of her beneficial effects. Von Hildebrand says that there is a third category of good specifically associated with people, that they have a value, a worth, even apart from my wants and needs.

I am free to evaluate my own actions using any of the three categories of good. In my own experience, I could see this when I taught an 8 a.m. Monday, Wednesday, and Friday ethics course. Ask any of my students at about 7:50 a.m. to evaluate the choice of sleeping in. On the pleasure scale, it ranks pretty high. On the good-for-you scale, it is the opposite. You can guess the result.

Evil is using the pleasure scale to evaluate people. For example, if I am heading to a great party, but I get a call from a friend considering suicide, I can either help him or not. I can choose to listen to the invitation of the party or the challenge of my friend's need:

> If we decide to help the person in great danger and thereby conform ourselves to the value and its challenge, we turn away from the attraction of the party ... If we decide instead to go to the promising social affair, we exclude the point of view of the value. In this struggle the respective victory is the victory of a general type of importance, and not only of a single real possibility.[33]

Using von Hildebrand's terminology, the eudaemonists have only one scale, happiness, which amounts to the second type of good. Given a single scale, it makes sense why nobody in their right mind would ever be able to choose what they know to be worse. Because we have the choice of scales, we can coldly and deliberately choose something we know to be worse on one scale (moral good) because it is higher on another (pleasure).

Like Kant, von Hildebrand would be a type of deontologist, but he believes that the purest motive is love rather than duty. For Kant, the highest motive is duty (and painful duty at that). The morally good person has mastered a kind of ruthless consistency of action. For von Hildebrand, the morally good person enjoys being good. Doing good is a love response to the value of the people around me; the more I respond, the more sensitive I become to their value, and the more I see value in others.[34]

I probably don't need to say that I think this is the most playable theory of evil so far. If I have an evil character, he or she does not have to be crazy or stupid or out of control with a pleasure addiction. At some point, the character made a choice, ignoring the value of the people around him to pursue some ambition. Over the years, repeating these sorts of choices led him to a point where he is largely blind to the worth of the people around him, caring only for his family and his party (if that). Now, the character thinks only of his own happiness when making any choice. As he sinks into evil, he becomes increasingly focused on himself and his appetites, which has the ironic effect of robbing him of the ability to enjoy the pleasures of life. A purely evil character is guilt-free but miserable.

Good characters can be interesting, too. Evil characters are ultimately interested in only one thing: satisfying their desires.

Good characters have the ability to focus on something bigger than themselves. They can dedicate themselves to a principle, a cause, or a person and sacrifice their own safety to support it. They can stick their necks out with little chance of gain. Because they can appreciate the worth of other people, they are also more interested in those around them.

Hannah Arendt and the Campaign of Evil

If you didn't know better, you would think that no woman ever played a role-playing game, judging by their packaging and themes (and by the existence of *Macho Women with Guns*). It's the same thing with philosophy. There have been women philosophers from the very beginning, from Diotima (c.400 BCE, chaotic good), who appears in Plato's *Symposium*, to St. Catherine of Alexandria (early fourth century, lawful good), who is the Catholic Church's "patron saint" of philosophy, to Edith Stein (1891–1942, neutral good), who was responsible for editing the early works of von Hildebrand's teacher, Edmund Husserl (1859–1938, lawful neutral) in addition to her own work on empathy and feminism.[35] However, it is only recently that being a respected philosophy professor and writer has been a real option for women, and so it is fitting that we have a woman running anchor for us.

Hannah Arendt (1906–75, chaotic good) is strangely tied with our other philosophers. She grew up in Kant's home town, and wrote extensively on the relationship of his theory of judgment to Aristotle's. She wrote her dissertation on Aquinas' hero, St. Augustine. In her later works, she used Socrates as her model of everyday ethics. She had a romantic relationship with philosopher Martin Heidegger (1889–1976, chaotic neutral), who studied under Husserl, von Hildebrand's teacher, and like von Hildebrand, she was forced to flee the Nazis and ended up teaching in the United States.

Arendt is best known for her political philosophy, particularly regarding totalitarianism. However, she developed her own system of ethics, with a unique conception of evil. Looking at the history of ethics, she reflected that concepts like happiness, courage, and justice are easy to recognize, but difficult to explain:

> These words ... are part and parcel of our everyday speech, and still we can give no account of them; when we try to define them, they get slippery; when we talk about their meaning, nothing stays put anymore, everything begins to move.[36]

Here we are, thousands of years after Socrates, still trying to figure out what happiness has to do with justice. There seems to be no hope that we will reach a point when this is no longer necessary.

Is that a problem? Arendt says no. Returning to Socrates (philosophers usually do), she notices that he never claimed to *know* anything. He considered his mission to be a gadfly, to wake people up by helping them to *think* so that they could be fully alive. He forced them to get rid of their unexamined prejudices. However, he did not do so to give them his own doctrine; rather, he often left them with only their perplexities.

This might sound like Arendt thinks that Socrates is a nihilist, someone who believes in nothing at all (yes, yes, I know you are thinking of *The Big Lebowski*,[37] but this is a *D&D* book). However, she actually claims that Socrates' approach is the only *antidote* to nihilism:

> Nihilism may be seen as an ever-present danger of thinking. But this danger does not arise out of the Socratic conviction that an unexamined life is not worth living but, on the contrary, out of the desire to find results which would make further thinking unnecessary.[38]

What does it mean to have an examined life? It means that there have to be times when I take a step back from my life and reflect on what it is all about. Thinking is a "habit of examining and reflecting upon whatever comes to pass."[39] This is not easy because in this world, "I am never alone and always much too busy to be able to think."[40] Thinking is a kind of love, a never-ending quest for meaning (the word *philosophy* means love of wisdom). As in any other quest, I desire my object, and so evil and ugliness are excluded from the thinking concern. Like any other love relationship, there is no end point, no point beyond which the quest is pointless. That is why we still reflect on the meaning of happiness, and that is why we will never stop.

Thinking is not the same as judgment, which is the ability to say "this is wrong," "this is beautiful," and so on. Judgment connects the abstract concepts of thinking and applies them to my particular circumstances. My busy daily life is a never-ending succession of judgments. If I lead an examined life, if I take time alone to think about what is invisible, I will be able to tell right from wrong. This will have a liberating effect on me, particularly "in the rare moments when the chips are down."[41]

Where do we get evil? "The sad truth of the matter," says Arendt, "is that most evil is done by people who never made up their mind to be either good or bad."[42] She said this after writing about the trial of Adolf Eichmann in Jerusalem in 1961. Eichmann was the lieutenant colonel tasked with managing the logistics of Hitler's concentration camps. In other words, he was personally in charge of the murder of five million human beings. While covering the trial, Arendt was shocked to find that Eichmann was not evil in any classical sense. He was an ordinary, commonplace man whom even the Israeli psychologists certified as normal. She uses the term "evil" to describe this as opposed to "wickedness":

> We were here not concerned with wickedness, with which religion and literature have tried to come to terms, but with evil; not with sin and the great villains who became the negative heroes in literature and usually acted out of envy and resentment, but with the non-wicked everybody who has no special motives and for this reason is capable of *infinite* evil; unlike the villain, he never meets his midnight disaster.[43]

The primary sources of evil are indifference and self-deception. Both lead me to a life of convention, simply living up to the code of conduct given to me by my society. Arendt says that most people live like this; "they get used to never making up their minds."[44] I get used to being given the rules by which I lead my life and make my own small decisions. The problem comes when the society giving me the rules happens to be Nazi Germany or Stalinist Russia. I can, like Eichmann, proceed to do my best to live up to expectations, even if that means doing things that I would have thought immoral if I had taken the time to reflect on it.

I hate to admit it, but I've got a problem with Arendt's analysis. As much as I love it (and I do), I cannot see how using it helps me play *D&D*. On one hand, this type of wrongdoing is specifically not purposeful. She says it herself: evil characters do not make good villains because they are just one of the "non-wicked everybody." On the other hand, who would want to play it? It would be a masterpiece of playing in character to be able to play a completely unremarkable person, but how long can you keep that up? Her evil characters are repellent, but not in a good way.

I've got an idea: the DM. We can keep her theory by using it as the paintbrush with which we paint the backdrop of our campaigns. How does a DM portray the average citizen of Ravenloft? The temptation is to make each one of them a wicked, mustache-twirling villain. However, they can be evil, completely ruled by the Dark Powers, but be rather normal people living their lives in an uninteresting way. We finally have a use for the "neutral" alignment!

End of Round

In my own education, I always wondered why this topic was so rarely discussed in ethics classes. I think Hannah Arendt's explanation is the best – we don't have much time to really *think*, and when we do, we don't want to spend our time thinking about what is ugly and bad. It is much more comfortable to think of evil as something done by villains in movies. There is something rather disturbing about the thought that one can become evil gradually. Once you realize that you can be evil without knowing it, you realize that *you can be evil without knowing it.*

Because of the influence of bad habits, much about the moral life feels grey and fuzzy. If you do find yourself in a clear moral situation once in a while, take advantage of it to do the right thing, because good habits are just as powerful. It may cost you some levels, and you may have to switch deities, but you will be – happy.

Notes

1. Richard Dawkins, "Faith and Reason." Interview. PBS, 1995. Available at http://www.pbs.org/faithandreason/transcript/dawk-body.html; accessed April 16, 2014.
2. J.L. Mackie, *Inventing Right and Wrong* (London: Penguin Books, 1991), p. 35.
3. John Stuart Mill, *Utilitarianism*, ch. 2.
4. Plato, *Apology*, 38a.
5. Plato, *Gorgias*, 494a.
6. Ibid., 507e.
7. Ibid., 467e.
8. Ibid., 499e.
9. Plato, *Protagoras*, 355e.
10. Plato, *Meno*, 89a.
11. Plato, *Protagoras*, 358b7–c1.
12. Aristotle, *Nicomachean Ethics*, Book I, ch. 7.
13. Ibid., Book VII, ch. 2.
14. Ibid.
15. Ibid., Book VII, ch. 3.
16. Ibid.
17. Ibid.
18. Thomas Aquinas, *Summa Contra Gentiles*, 3, 25.
19. Augustine of Hippo, *De nupt. et concup.*, II, xxvi, 43.
20. Thomas Aquinas, *Summa Theologiae*, I-II, q. 78, a. 1.
21. Ibid., a. 2.
22. Cf. Philip H. Wicksteed, *Dante & Aquinas* (London: J. M. Dent & Sons, 1913).

23. Immanuel Kant, *Critique of Practical Reason*, trans. Thomas Kingsmill (Amherst, NY: Prometheus Books, 1996), Pt. I, Bk. I, ch. 2.

24. Immanuel Kant, *Groundwork of the Metaphysic of Morals*, trans. H.J. Paton (New York: Harper & Row, 1964), opening of ch. 1.

25. *Critique of Practical Reason*, Pt. I, Bk. I, ch. 7.

26. Ibid., ch. 3.

27. Immanuel Kant, *Religion Within the Boundaries of Mere Reason*, trans. Allen Wood (Cambridge: Cambridge University Press, 1998), 6:30.

28. Ibid.

29. Ibid., 6:58.

30. John F. Crosby, "The Witness of Dietrich Von Hildebrand," *First Things*. Available at http://www.firstthings.com/article/2007/01/the-witness-of-dietrich-von-hildebrand, accesses April 16, 2014.

31. Dietrich Von Hildebrand, *Ethics* (Chicago: Franciscan Herald Press, 1953), p. 23.

32. Ibid., p. 31.

33. Ibid., p. 42.

34. Ibid., p. 221.

35. Cf. Marianne Sawicki, "Personal Connections: The Phenomenology of Edith Stein," Lecture, St. John's University, New York, 12 Dec. 2012. Hesburgh Libraries, University of Notre Dame. Available at http://library.nd.edu/colldev/subject_home_pages/catholic/personal_connections.shtml; accessed April 16, 2014.

36. Hannah Arendt, "Thinking and Moral Considerations." *Social Research* 38 (1971), p. 429.

37. See Peter J. Fosl, ed., *The Big Lebowski and Philosophy: Keeping Your Mind Limber with Abiding Wisdom* (Hoboken, NJ: Wiley, 2012).

38. Arendt, "Thinking and Moral Considerations," p. 435.

39. Ibid., p. 418.

40. Ibid., p. 446.

41. Ibid.

42. Ibid., p. 438.

43. Ibid., p. 445.

44. Ibid., p. 436.

Part II

SO DID YOU WIN? PHILOSOPHY AND *D&D* GAMEPLAY

Save vs. Death

Some Reflections on the Lifecycle of PCs

Christopher Robichaud

The first edition of the *Player's Handbook* (1978). Page 23. Know what's on it? If you're an old school guy like me, you surely do: David Sutherland's famous illustration, "A Paladin in Hell." We see a holy warrior, wearing full plate mail, standing atop a precipice, swinging his sword into the shoulder of a devil. Blood flies. But more devils line up to attack the paladin. And no doubt more will come after them. And then more. It is hell, after all. There is an *endless* supply of devils.

The paladin is going to die.

Oh, I know. This is *Dungeons & Dragons*. A magic-user might come to save the day with a potent spell. A cleric's prayers might lead to the intervention of a god. Perhaps the sword the paladin is wielding is an artifact with a *get the hell out of hell* power.

Maybe. But I can't shake the feeling that we're witnessing the paladin's last stand. He (or she; we'll never really know) won't go down without a fight, of course. What paladin would? And believe it or not, the devils aren't going to lay a finger on him thanks to his *protection from evil* aura, which in this first edition of the game (ah, yes, here comes some good 'ol game-breakage) emanates perpetually from the paladin no matter what he does.

Dungeons & Dragons and Philosophy: Read and Gain Advantage on All Wisdom Checks, First Edition. Edited by Christopher Robichaud.
© 2014 John Wiley & Sons, Inc. Published 2014 by John Wiley & Sons, Inc.

Eventually, though, the paladin is going to starve, or fall to his death, or stumble upon one of those nasty arch-devils in the *Monster Manual* who are just going to throw some high-level magic the paladin's way that will surely ruin his plans for level advancement.

In other words, the paladin is going to die.

"So what?" you might ask. He gets to go out in a blaze of glory fit for a holy warrior. Except not really. The paladin is in *hell*. He can kill a thousand devils before dying and it's not going to make a dent in the population. He's not going to make this plane any better by sword or prayer or charity. If anything, he'll amuse the greater powers who call this lawful evil domain their home until one way or the other, he drops. Then they'll eat his corpse, after desecrating it. That's it.

Whoever's character this is, the player is about to confront one of the uglier parts of the game: the unsatisfying death of a PC.

Death Be Not Proud

Ugly? Yes. For some *D&D* players, the death of a beloved character, especially if that death isn't heroic, is like losing a dear friend. That might make some people squirm and worry about us gamers, but hear me out. In *D&D*, unlike video games, it typically takes years and years to advance your character to levels of significance. At least that's the case with the older editions. If your character managed to survive those early levels, where you had him work very hard at avoiding most combat encounters, stealing – excuse me, acquiring – gold for experience points, then you had much to be proud of. Later levels brought better treasure, greater power, and more opportunity for heroics – at high risk.

And it's the risk that will eventually do most PCs in. I'm not talking about calculated risks, like a group of adventurers deciding that it's better to enter the dragon's lair by day rather than by night, after spending some time in the accompanying towns gaining insight into the dragon's hunting habits. I'm talking about the inevitable risks that the game brings with it, those moments when despite the best strategy, you find yourself rolling a saving throw for your character that's going to be the difference between him soaking up that acid breath weapon damage or him being liquefied. And sometimes, no matter what the odds are, you just get unlucky. In *D&D*, no matter how powerful you are, most every time you roll that D20, you have at least a 5 percent chance of things going very badly for a beloved character.

It's one of the reasons why I love the game.

No, really, it's true. I miss earlier editions. Later editions got rid of, or at least significantly nerfed, the save vs. something awful rolls. These are the all-or-nothing moments in the game. Your character turned a corner and found himself staring at a medusa. Bummer. It doesn't much matter that he's 15th level, does it? Save vs. petrification or now he's a 15th-level piece of stone. You made that save? Good. Oh, look at that. Lucky roll by the Dungeon Master. The medusa has managed to hit your character with her tail. Save vs. poison or he dies.

In Plato's (c.429–c.347 BCE) *Phaedo*, the character Socrates tells us that there is no better preparation for death than living the life of a philosopher. Happily, I've got that base covered. But the thing is, I think Socrates was wrong, though he couldn't have known it at the time. Turns out there is no better preparation for thinking about death – or just as importantly, for thinking about many of the important features of life – than regularly playing *D&D*.

Before I get to that, though, let's at least briefly hear Socrates out.

Phaedo and Confronting the Reaper

In *Phaedo*, Socrates has already been found guilty of corrupting the youth and teaching people not to believe in the gods. His punishment: death by drinking hemlock. During his final hours, Socrates tells his friends why he doesn't fear death, but rather, looks forward to it. Moreover, he thinks this is the only reasonable attitude a philosopher can have, since philosophy prepares us for death.

According to Socrates, the life of philosophy is a life of the mind. Or as he would likely put it, a life of the soul. The philosopher, on his view, goes out of his way to eschew physical pleasures and materialistic pursuits. He works hard at not indulging in pleasures of the flesh, rich diets, or luxuries of any sort. And he does this for a reason. True knowledge is knowledge of the Forms – Justice, Beauty, Truth – you know, the big stuff. Our ability to gain knowledge of this sort is thwarted by the distractions of the body and of materialistic goods. Philosophers, therefore, cultivate a practice of pursuing knowledge of the Forms through disengagement from the physical, to the extent that's possible.

What does this have to do with death, though? Death, according to Socrates, is "separation of the soul from the body."[1] The soul persists, while the body does not. And this is precisely what philosophers have been aiming at. So: win! They have tried throughout their lives to keep the soul unencumbered by the body in order to gain knowledge. Death finally allows that to happen completely. Rather than fear death, then, we should embrace it. At least if we are philosophers, Socrates thinks.

If Socrates is right, though, I'm in trouble. I am indeed a philosopher, but I'm also a gamer, and like most gamers, I start getting awful grumpy if you suggest that I should give up my Mountain Dew and various 7-11 snacks at the table. Happily, we have reason to be suspicious of Socrates' reasoning. Knowledge doesn't require disengagement from the body, but just the opposite. Those of us standing in the empiricist tradition see most knowledge stemming precisely from the bodily senses. Just ask the philosopher David Hume (1711–76). We learn about the world around us by observing it, hypothesizing about it, and then testing it. This is how ordinary knowledge is gained, like knowing that I have a hand. It's also how scientific knowledge is gained. Even mathematical knowledge – the most abstract knowledge there is – doesn't require the kind of bodily disengagement Socrates describes.

As far as the question of whether death is best conceived as a kind of immortal soul disengaging from a physical body, that, alas, is a subject too rich to explore at present. What can be said is that even if true, there isn't quite as much comfort to be taken from it as Socrates imagines. For one thing, one's immortal soul might end up in a very good place – think the Seven Heavens – or a very bad place – think the Nine Hells. For another, if philosophers – and others – can gain plenty of knowledge about the world with our body and souls intertwined, and it sure seems that we can, then death doesn't achieve any interesting philosophical goals, at least from an epistemological standpoint.

The Graveyard of Dead PCs

So I don't think Socrates, brilliant though he was, had much to offer us in terms of thinking about death. But I do think playing *D&D* does. A bold claim, to be sure. Let's start exploring it, dungeon-crawl style.

I'm a big fan of *I6: Ravenloft*. Flaws and all, it's consistently ranked among the best *D&D* modules of all time. And rightly so, for a hundred reasons, including those great "little touches." The one I'm thinking about now is the description of the cemetery in the village of Barovia.

> Every night at midnight … a ghostly procession takes place. One hundred spirits march up the road to Castle Ravenloft … At the castle, the spirits march straight to the chapel … up the high tower stair … to the top of the tower … There, they throw themselves down the shaft toward the crypts, where they disappear. These are the spirits of previous adventurers who died trying to destroy Strahd. Every night they try to complete their quest and each night they fail.[2]

What a bleak afterlife! But then, just about everything in the cursed lands of Barovia is bleak, and remains so as long as the land is in thrall to "the devil" Strahd, master vampire.

Still, this fantastic image offers us a way to think about the death of our characters. A very tempting way, but ultimately misguided, I think. When that saving throw is missed for your monk against the wail of the banshee roaming the halls of Castle Ravenloft; when that police robot (yes, that's right) hangs more damage on your druid with that incendiary grenade than you ever thought possible in *S3: Expedition to the Barrier Peaks*; when your master thief "scouts ahead" through the green devil face in *S1: Tomb of Horrors* and is annihilated instantaneously – no saving throw, because, well, because Gygax; when all the *raise dead* and *resurrection* spells are exhausted and you're still looking at a very bad number on your sacred D20 – the one you sleep with under your pillow at night; when the character you spent years and years developing is dead and he's not coming back, that's a pivotal moment in *D&D* gameplay.

You could have a complete emotional breakdown. There's no shame in it. Plenty of us have. You could spend weeks going over the bad roll and envisioning your beloved fighter or cleric or magic-user or what-have-you now as a cursed member of the graveyard of dead PCs, doomed forever to try, and of course fail, to complete the one quest that undid him. You could imagine yourself a paladin who's stuck in hell, eternally fighting an infinite number of devils, making no progress. You could do that, and I would be a little surprised if Tracy and Laura Hickman weren't very aware of tapping into that sentiment when describing the cemetery in Barovia.

Alternatively, you could just pull out a blank piece of paper, roll up another PC, and jump back into the game.

PCs die. 1st-level PCs die. 18th-level PCs die. And much of it is due simply to the roll of a die. But the game goes on, with you as part of it, so long as you're ready to roll up another character and jump back in. *That* is the essence of *D&D*. I promised some life and death philosophical lessons from playing the game. The first is this: play at life passionately, but be detached enough to let go when the dice don't roll in your favor. Passion and detachment, in living life and confronting death. That's not an original philosophical idea, of course. It finds a welcome home from various strands of Buddhist thought; indeed, the idea I'm pointing to is captured exceptionally well in the Tibetan Buddhist tradition of creating sand mandalas. These are created with much passion, rigor, creativity and sophistication. They are also left to blow away, and when that doesn't happen, are consciously swept aside. Buddhists in this tradition put much significance in this process. For them, it reveals a *fundamental* truth about life, death, and the impermanence connecting the two.

Ability Scores: The Natural Lottery

Suppose, then, you take this idea to heart. Let go of that PC. Retire the sheet and roll up a new character. Wait! Time for the second big philosophical lesson in the lifecycle of PCs. It's this: just as with player-characters, our natural advantages and dis-advantages are due to luck.

This, no doubt, seems obvious on the PC side of things, given that the characters' strengths and weaknesses are determined by rolling six-sided dice. Actually, if we're being honest, when we start thinking about rolling up characters, we immediately start graphing probabilities based on the various methods described in the *Dungeon Master's Guide*. Let's push past that, for all of our sakes. The ability scores of a character are his spine, and everything hangs off of them. Strength, dexterity, constitution, intelligence, wisdom, and charisma: these hallowed traits are the foundation upon which everything else about a character is built. Something so important couldn't really be determined by random dice rolls, could it? In the older editions of the game, the answer is an emphatic yes.

You play what you roll. Didn't get the scores you needed for a ranger? It's okay. There's always the fighter. You know how it goes. Rolled poorly on your hit points? Be careful! You're as squishy as the wizard. The lucky and unlucky rolls at the character-creation stage give the player advantages and disadvantages – all unearned. Her skill comes in how she works with them.

The philosophical insight is that the same is true with us. It may not sound all that insightful at first. *Of course* our natural talents – our height, intelligence, beauty, and so on – were not things we earned, or deserve, but were determined by a "natural lottery" – a cosmic rolling of some six-sided dice. So what? It turns out that for some philosophers, this fact of life has some rather important implications.

John Rawls (1921–2002) built a portion of his theory of political justice upon the idea that our natural talents are not earned, but acquired by luck. Rawls was concerned with what would make a state just – what political and economic institutions it needed to establish in order to count as promoting justice. And one of his principles of justice stated that society ought to be arranged in such a way that inequalities of income and wealth could only be justified to the extent that they maximized the welfare of those people in society occupying the worst-off positions. This *difference principle* – as it has come to be called – is rather demanding, and its satisfaction would likely require the state to adopt policies that significantly redistribute wealth.[3]

For a lot of people in America, this idea is anathema. And the argument against it goes something like this. The money we earn from our labor is earned from, well, *our* labor. We have a special claim on it, a claim that's violated if the government adopts policies that tax the fruits of our labor to redistribute it to others. This idea, in very rough form, is the foundation of much libertarian thought.[4]

Rawls, however, has a rejoinder, based squarely on the observation that our natural talents were a matter of luck. As he sees it, we don't have an absolute claim on the fruits of our labor because not all of those fruits are *deserved*. Yes, we developed skills. But no matter how skillful we are, we need certain natural talents to succeed at some things. And those we didn't earn. They just came to us. Through luck. A player's fighter may earn an extra 10 percent in experience points due to a high strength score, but since that score was the result of a roll of the dice, the player shouldn't pat herself on the back for earning it. She didn't do anything but roll dice. If a DM decided to distribute those extra experience points to the poor guy who rolled a bunch of 3s on his ability scores, what claim would the player have against the DM – besides pounding on the relevant page in the book? (And we all know how those arguments go.)

For Rawls, then, we don't have an *absolute* claim on the fruits of our labor because not all of them are earned. Now, admittedly there is a lot more to say about this, but the take-home insight is this: the reality of luck may carry with it obligations of justice. And if that's not deep, we've been delving together in the wrong dungeon.

We've talked about how the death of a PC can be an invitation to think about passion and detachment, and how the creation of a new PC can be an invitation to think about fairness and justice. Does playing *D&D* really lend itself to thinking about such things? Of course! And we've just gotten to level 1. This is Undermountain. There's *always* further down to go.

Notes

1. From *The Last Days of Socrates*, trans. Hugh Tredennick (Harmondsworth: Penguin Classics, 1954), 67d.
2. Tracy Hickman and Laura Hickman, *I6: Ravenloft* (Lake Geneva, WI: Tactical Studies Rules, 1983).
3. Rawls develops this position in *Theory of Justice* (Cambridge, MA: Harvard University Press, 1971).
4. For more on this, see Robert Nozick's *Anarchy, State and Utopia* (New York: Basic Books, 1974).

5

To My Other Self
Reflection and Existentialism in *Dungeons & Dragons*

Rob Crandall and Charles Taliaferro

The most interesting *Dungeons & Dragons* phenomenon is not in a rulebook – it is in my head.[1] It is what happens when I become Nascen, Soren, Rylavan, Yui, Sayir-Sorashana, or Volkra. For during that time, I am someone else: I am a mad wizard, a beguiling ghost, or a fire-breathing barbarian. I think, speak, and act as a person who does not exist and will never exist, except in my mind.

Of course, the replacement is not complete. I can "take control" of myself at any time – or even refuse to become this other person at all. We all know the type – the person whose character concept is limited to a class and race. Role-playing is not everyone's cup of tea, after all, and removing it leaves *D&D* a perfectly serviceable game. To those of you who don't care for role-playing: this chapter may not be for you. To those of you who don't care for role-playing but do care for introspection, however: read on. The two are more closely tied than you may have thought.

This is the point of games such as *Dungeons & Dragons*. The player assumes a role as a power fantasy or wish-fulfillment, so that they may pretend to be someone else, someone who can do

Dungeons & Dragons and Philosophy: Read and Gain Advantage on All Wisdom Checks, First Edition. Edited by Christopher Robichaud.
© 2014 John Wiley & Sons, Inc. Published 2014 by John Wiley & Sons, Inc.

things that the player can only dream of. Certainly, this is some-what true – and, as a quick mental exercise, let's consider it. Do you have a favorite role? A favorite archetype? Rogues are a popular one, in particular the type of rogue who steals every-thing that isn't nailed down (sometimes including things that belong to other party members). Perhaps you, or someone you know, plays characters who consistently bear a resemblance to a specific fictional character. The 3.5 *Dungeon Master's Guide II* sourcebook discusses player motivations such as these, recog-nizing that, for many, they are one of the main reasons to play *D&D*. Three of the particular motivations of this nature that it calls out are playing a favorite archetype, "supercoolness," and irresponsibility: three motivations which all represent the desire to experience something that the person can't have, at least not to the same degree, in real life.[2]

Just from this, you can form some conclusions, at least about your fellow players. Doing so is easy and natural. The strong, uncomplicated fellow likes to play fighters? We laugh. Of *course* he does, we wouldn't have expected anything else. We would be surprised indeed to learn of anyone making his or her first *D&D* character a member of a class that did not in some way reflect his or her own personality – unless, of course, the party needed a member of that class. A character's class, at least free from the constraints of other party members' choices, is representative of what the player finds most appealing about a world like the one *D&D* offers. Is it magic? Play a wizard, or one of the many other spellcasting classes. Is it the idea of noble heroes, striving valiantly against the forces of evil? A paladin will do. And so on, for everything that a class can represent and everything a player can desire. We unconsciously see these archetypes bringing traits of our fellow players to the foreground, but it takes some reflec-tion to see it in ourselves. What are the meanings of these arche-types? That is for you to decide.

This, however, barely touches the surface of what we can learn about ourselves through *D&D*. Whereas a character's class will inevitably depend on preferred edition, house rules, and so on, role-playing itself – history, goals, fears – is the heart of a character, with the added attraction of being portable between editions. The depth of a character, and what can be found in those depths, is far more revealing.

The Actor, the Author, and the Other

What I am describing is familiar to anyone who has performed in a play. Actors are encouraged to not only speak and act as their characters, but also to think and feel as them. Spending hours a day in someone else's head certainly changes the way that you perceive yourself! But an actor's character is (except in rare cases) not their own. The actor plays a character that someone else has envisioned and written: a figment of someone else's imagination. Contrast this to *D&D*, where (except in rare cases) a role-player's character is their own. It is a person that they have shaped and are now, every minute, bringing to life.

The author's task looks at the other side of this coin: an author conceives of a world and characters, then sees how those characters will react to their circumstances. To some extent, the author must think as the character, but an author has a luxury that an actor lacks – time. The words spoken by a character in a novel or a play can be revised, rewritten, edited; entire conversations can be inserted or excised. Until the paper hits the presses, events can change at any time. Compare that to your DM's policy on "takebacks:" you will likely find a shocking difference. Authors who write in the third person also have the luxury of distance. They must watch their characters, but they need not become them, and the simple pronoun substitution can vastly change the perspectives of both writer and reader.

Role-playing, then, is neither simply creation of a character nor simply acting. So what happens when I play my character? I cannot simply think as myself, or I do an injustice to the richness of what my character could be. But I cannot be someone else; this is simply impossible. I am fundamentally incapable of knowing what another person would think or do in my situation, so I must settle for a variation on what I would do. Since I cannot be someone else, what I do instead – what I must do – is to create a framework of *otherness*, a series of lenses and prisms through which I filter my thoughts. The pieces of this scaffolding are the components of my character.

This is really not that different from what we do every day. Although I may have known a friend for many years, I can never know what he is thinking, nor can I ever claim, with certainty, that he will take a specific action – at least, assuming that I believe in free will. I cannot predict what he will say or do because he is something fundamentally alien to me: he is the Other, in the words of philosopher Jean-Paul Sartre (1905–1980). If I am to assume that the world makes any sense, I must believe that other human beings will act in a way that has what I can recognize as purpose and reason. But the only reasoning mind I can be certain of, absolutely, is my own. So I have to assume that my reason is adequate to stretch itself and accommodate the differing circumstances of a friend, a relative, or a spouse, and that, once I have taken those differences into account, I can approximate what another person would think.

In Word and Deed

For whose benefit do you make a deep, multidimensional character? Who gains the most from it? To some extent, this depends on your DM and your campaign. If the campaign calls for political intrigue and focuses on non-combat interactions, then the creation of a well-defined character will help not only you but also your fellow players and the DM. A caricature feels out of place beside a gallery of convincing characters and spoils, if not the immersion of the campaign, at least its mood. If the campaign is not focused primarily or exclusively on role-playing, others may still appreciate having someone who's thought out a character with them (in particular the Dungeon Master; a deeper character means more material to work with). But it is equally likely that your fellow players will find a character who talks a lot and tries to reason with the bandits instead of simply fireball-slinging a nuisance rather than an asset. Fundamentally, then, the one for whom I make my character is myself.

This raises the point, however, of how we perceive others' characters, and how they perceive ours. I have seen characters with backstories spanning decades and pages who are, nevertheless, reduced to a single sentence in the eyes of their comrades. I may have constructed the framework I have described above and brought my character to life within my own mind. But if I do not portray that at the table, does it mean anything? In the end, that character is defined by his or her actions and words, not by my thoughts. All of the good intention in the world does not absolve a character of accusations of backstabbing the party – nor does all the bad luck in the world absolve a character of accusations of incompetence.

This, again, finds an echo in Sartre's writing. In his essay "Existentialism," he states that the core of existential philosophy is that "Man is nothing else than his plan; he exists only to the extent that he fulfills himself; he is therefore nothing else than the ensemble of his acts, nothing else than his life."[3] Sartre rightly identifies that this seems horrific to many, who would prefer to think of themselves as including their unrealized potential. But even if we grant that this dictum may not apply to actual human beings, it is much harder to refute for fictional characters. The characters of a book have no existence independent of how the author describes them, their words, and their actions. Similarly, the character you role-play has no existence apart from what she does at the table. What you have your character say and do *is* the character – and while it is possible that how others see your character is different from your own mental image, or your original conception, this is simply art mirroring life.

Mirror and Illusion

Perhaps my character is a cleric; perhaps an atheist (or perhaps even an atheist cleric). Perhaps he or she has a vastly different background from my own, or is a member of a race with social mores strikingly different from those of twenty-first-century suburban America. I will look at history, aspirations, and personality. Each of these is a fragment of my character's identity and a point where his or her thoughts will differ from my own. These, whatever edition of *D&D* you prefer, are the universal building blocks of a character. Classes, feats, armor class (AC), saves (or defenses) are all incidental to the central concept; I can build Soren Altigo as easily in fourth edition as in 3.5, and he will still be the same character, even if his class changes.

Once these foundations have been laid down, I must bring the character to life. When role-playing, I lack the luxuries of time and a script to work from: I must be able to respond to anything the Dungeon Master hurls partyward more or less instantly. What I say goes, and it will stay around to define my character in the eyes of the party. So I keep this scaffolding in my mind, and carry it around with me. But thinking in this way, for hours at a time, and simply bearing the idea of that character around, must change me. It will cause me to think about things in ways I have not before, or pay attention to thoughts I would have otherwise not heeded.

When I am an amoral drow warlock for four hours every night, I may regard the world around me with more detachment and cynicism; when I am a psychic soldier on Friday evenings, I may find myself emphasizing self-discipline and restraint in my daily life. This may sound slightly delusional, particularly if you describe it to someone who hasn't acted or played *D&D*, but it is true nonetheless. When I spend energy and time filtering my thoughts, even on specific occasions, it will filter out into my everyday life, if only to a small degree.

The player, then, creates the character, who then influences the player. In playing characters, we converse with ourselves: every sentence spoken by our characters is addressed, in a way, to ourselves, and every action taken the by our characters is directed at ourselves. Of course, many of these are wish-fulfillment. Courage, after all, is easy when you are sitting in a comfortable chair, surrounded by your friends. But aside from the obvious examples of such fantasy, this sort of dialogue can teach us much, particularly since every virtue a character displays, every noble deed, has its origins in the player. Although the thoughts of the player are filtered into the character, the character can never take an action that is completely beyond the comprehension of the player. Now, this applies not only to virtues, but vices as well. A player whose character takes too much glee in the near-inevitable slaughter that occurs in most campaigns may be someone to watch out for! On the other hand, the player may simply be channeling centuries of cultural history – but that's a different discussion. The relevant issue here is that, in playing characters, we can become aware of virtues we did not know we had until we saw them embodied in our characters.

Experience without EXP

All of this discussion leaves out, however, the organic nature of a character. Many characters are flat, and end the campaign no different than they started it, albeit richer and more deadly than some small nations. But to accept this as inevitable is to portray a caricature rather than a character. After all, we expect growth and development from the heroes of any other narrative form, so we should accept, if not expect, that D&D characters can show something similar. I must confess that seeing my character, and those of others, change over the course of the story, and seeing how their endings are different from their beginnings, has always been my favorite part of a campaign. Of course, I'm not only referring to the accumulation of powers, feats, skills, and loot, but of lessons, influences, and drastic, life-changing events. What effect do these have on the player?

If hosting another person within one's head has a psychological effect (and it does; just ask a kalashtar), then seeing that person become something else must have a profound effect indeed. Perhaps the DM throws the unexpected at your party, and something you never could have anticipated takes your character by surprise. Perhaps it was your plan all along that your whoring cleric would find love and settle down, but perhaps it was simply a whim you conceived of for him when he met the right woman. As long as it makes sense for the character, a spur-of-the-moment idea is no less valid than a pages-long life plan – given the traditional propensity of most DMs for upsetting carefully laid plans, it may be more valid, or at least easier to realize!

Moments such as these are the real test of a character and the real chances for a player to explore the meaning of that character to him or her. A fully realized character will be able to emerge from such crises stronger, perhaps changed irrevocably. Attempts to teach less realized characters lessons will make less impact on them than snow on a white dragon. Again, I stress: this is not an invalid way of playing *D&D*, nor is it an inferior one. We all want different things from our entertainment, and working through the impact of events on someone's nature isn't what everyone likes to do in their spare time.

For those who are willing to look into their character and internalize the impact of such events, however, they are an invaluable experience for both the character and the player. The character learns and changes, and the player learns both more about the character she has created and about herself. This is when a character, in a sense, can finally detach from the player and stand on her own. The DM (or another player) has thrown an alien element into the scaffolding of the character, and the character must react – again, without the luxury of time to ponder the implications fully. No, the player must determine *now* how this has affected her character.

This is possibly the most valuable piece of introspection that *D&D* can provide. The original concept of a character is within the player's more or less complete control, but the events of the campaign are not. And so we learn lessons about who we are: about how we handle power, betrayal, disappointment, and loss. To the extent that you truly portray your character and allow him or her to grow, particularly in ways you never anticipated, you learn about yourself.

Every character has a bit – or a lot – of the player in them. With every character I make, I bring a new side of myself to the foreground, for the examination of myself and of others. And in doing so, I learn more about myself, and about my fellow players who are doing the same. In *The Myth of Sisyphus*, the seminal existentialist writer Albert Camus (1913–60) writes:

> It is certain that apparently, though I have seen the same actor a hundred times, I shall not for that reason know him any better personally. Yet if I add up all the heroes he has personified and if I say that I know him a little better at the hundredth character counted off, this will be felt to contain an element of truth ... A man defines himself by his make-believe as well as by his sincerest impulses.[4]

One almost wonders if Camus predicted *Dungeons & Dragons*. Camus, like other existentialists, means something slightly different by the final sentence than we might assume. When he states that "a man defines himself by his make-believe as well as by his sincerest impulses," he means exactly that: that in pretending, in acting, a man shapes how he sees himself and how others see him – in others words, who he is. This is the heart of the philosophy behind role-playing: it is that in defining our characters, we define ourselves, to whatever slight degree those characters embody us, mold us, or make us think or feel something different from what we see in our everyday lives. If I played *D&D* from now until the end of time (I can think of far worse fates), and someone could see all of the characters I played, perhaps that person would have a complete understanding of me, for I would have defined who I am in front of his or her eyes.

Role-playing is, after all, only make-believe. But in that make-believe, we can still feel, still think – and is an emotion any less true because its object is only, in the end, illusion? The emotion is still true, and if I find something true about myself by looking into an illusionary mirror, it is no less true for its source. When I make a character, I see myself; when I play a character, I shape myself. This is no falsehood – I can speak from the experience of the characters I have played. This very chapter owes its existence to one from whom I learned that I had the capacity for courage and faith, to Lady Yui – to my other self.

Notes

1. This chapter is a collaborative work, but all first-person accounts refer to Rob Crandall.
2. Jesse Decker, David Noonan, et al., *Dungeon Master's Guide II* (Renton, WA: Wizards of the Coast, 2005), pp. 13–15.
3. Jean-Paul Sartre, "Existentialism," in Gordon Marino, ed., *Basic Writings of Existentialism* (New York: Random House, 2004), p. 355.
4. Albert Camus, "The Myth of Sisyphus," in Gordon Marino, ed., *Basic Writings of Existentialism* (New York: Random House, 2004), p. 447.

Player-Character Is What You Are in the Dark
The Phenomenology of Immersion in *Dungeons & Dragons*

William J. White

The idea of role-playing makes some people nervous – even some people who play role-playing games (RPGs). *Yeah, sure, we pretend to be wizards and talk in funny voices,* such players often say. *So what? It's just for fun. It's not like it* means *anything.* These players tend to find talk about role-playing games being "art" to be pretentious nonsense, and the idea that there could be philosophical value in a game like *Dungeons & Dragons* strikes them as preposterous on its face. "RPGs as instruction on ethics or metaphysics?" writes one such player in an online forum for discussing role-playing games. "Utter intellectualoid [*sic*] bullshit…[from those] who want to imagine they're great thinkers thinking great thoughts while they play RPGs because they'd otherwise feel ashamed about pretending to be an elf."[1]

By the same token, people who don't play RPGs are often quite mystified about what could possibly be going on in a game of *Dungeons & Dragons: There's no board? How do you win? No winners? Then why do you* play?[2] Making sense of *D&D* as an experience can require a good deal of mental effort on the part of the uninitiated, perhaps because of how RPGs weave together the concepts of *story* and *game* in an unfamiliar way.

But it is exactly that weaving together that makes *Dungeons & Dragons* interesting from a philosophical standpoint. Philosopher Kendall Walton argues that representation in fictional works has always proceeded from a playful or "ludic" orientation.[3] All fiction is a game of make-believe, so the first narrative form to make that connection explicit (as RPGs do) is necessarily worth exploring. And the foregrounding of *game* over *story* that begins with the tabletop RPG carries over to *D&D*-inspired digital and online games as well as electronic literature more broadly. Understanding how *Dungeons & Dragons* does what it does can provide insight into the operation of what some are calling *participatory culture*,[4] meaning that sort of industrious fandom in which the activity of the audience is more than mere reception, but an active and productive engagement with popular culture. From this perspective, *D&D* shares an important feature with writing Harry Potter fan fiction, playing *World of Warcraft*, and dressing up for *Twilight* cosplay: all of these instances of participatory culture facilitate an immersive engagement with a fictional setting through the lens of character. If we can explain *immersion*, in other words, then we can talk about role-playing in general and *Dungeons & Dragons* in particular in a way that both the novice and the skeptical "grognard" (old-school player) can appreciate.

The Idea of Immersion Leads to Phenomenology

So the idea of immersion is central to understanding how *Dungeons & Dragons* and other aspects of participatory culture work. Indeed, it can be argued that "immersion is to the 21st-century entertainment industry what illusion was to that of the 20th."[5] Game designers and social scientists alike have spent a great deal of time trying to figure out what immersion is, how it operates, and how to achieve it. Immersion is a sprawling concept, understood as having to do with being engrossed in the play of a game, or identifying strongly with a character in a story, or feeling as if one were in some sense present in an imaginary setting, for example. It is sometimes associated with psychologist Michael Csikszentmihalyi's concept of "flow," in which "optimal experience" is achieved when an undertaking challenges but doesn't overwhelm us.[6] Discussions of immersion among gamers can at times be heated, because of the varying and incompatible definitions held by different people.[7]

The one thing that *isn't* responsible for immersion, according to game design gurus Katie Salen and Eric Zimmerman, is the increasingly realistic representation of an imaginary setting by technological means – even though some game developers talk as if this were the case. For example, a bit of this view can be seen even in digital media professor Janet Murray's definition of immersion as "the experience of being transported to *an elaborately simulated place*" (emphasis added).[8] Salen and Zimmerman call this the "immersive fallacy," and argue that immersion is located instead in the minds of the players, in their experience of play, rather than in the technological sophistication, verisimilitude, the "realism" of the medium.[9] Once we begin to see immersion as a function of the game-player's subjective experience, rather than of the technical means used to create that experience, the door is opened to a *phenomenological approach* to immersion.

What Is Phenomenology?

Phenomenology is a kind of "philosophy of mind" associated with the works of twentieth-century philosophers Edmund Husserl (1859–1938), Martin Heidegger (1889–1976), Jean-Paul Sartre (1905–80), and Maurice Merleau-Ponty (1908–61), among others. The word "phenomenology," coined by Husserl, depends upon the sense of the word "phenomenon" that means "appearances" or "perceptions," since phenomenology is interested in the world as it is perceived, or "things as they appear in our experience."[10]

The purpose of phenomenology is to describe what it is like to be conscious or to have a given experience. To the phenomenological perspective, "all problems amount to finding definitions of essences,"[11] which means that the accounts of lived consciousness that the phenomenologist creates are presented as general descriptions of categories of experience – their essence, that is to say – rather than reconstructions of specific events. The domain of phenomenology encompasses the entire range of experiences in the world, paying attention to what Husserl called "intentionality," or how our consciousness is directed toward particular objects in the world. All consciousness, we are told repeatedly by the phenomenological philosophers, is consciousness *of* something. Phenomenology is thus a sort of *reflexive consciousness*, a consciousness of consciousness.

So the phenomenologist would ask, *What is it like to role-play?* or *What is it like to be immersed in a role-playing game?* The first step in most phenomenological analysis is a sort of attitude check called the *epoche*, or reduction of the "natural attitude" (i.e., the "general positing of existence" that presumes there is a real world that determines what is experienced). This involves *bracketing* the question of what is "real" or what is "really there" in favor of focusing on describing the individual's subjective, lived experience, without stipulating anything about their reality or irreality. Jean-Paul Sartre says "This procedure is…a 'step back' from belief concerning what exists in nature…. In 'stepping backward' one does not contest any factual belief…. Rather, one 'steps back', as it were, from the 'natural viewpoint' of factual belief."[12] Phenomenology is thus *agnostic* about the nature of reality; as Sartre says, "little importance is attached to whether the individual fact which serves as underpinning to the essence is real or imaginary."[13]

Having made this reduction or *epoche*, the phenomenologist then interrogates the data, which in classical phenomenology was usually the personal experience of the phenomenologist. Today phenomenological assumptions and approaches have been adopted by researchers in sociology, psychology, anthropology, and communication studies. So, they may include all manner of qualitative (descriptive) sources, such as "interviews, conversations, participant observation, action research, focus meetings, and analysis of personal texts."[14] This "interrogation" amounts to looking for recurring themes, patterns, or motifs in the way that the experience is described, focusing on the act of experiencing or the perception of phenomena.

In our case, we are interested in examining accounts of playing *Dungeons & Dragons* for what they suggest about the nature or character of immersion. For data, we'll use published accounts of play from a variety of sources – memoirs, short stories, magazine articles, online discussions, and scholarly essays – to see what common elements emerge, and how they contribute to a notion of immersion.

Seeing Is Believing: Immersion as Visualization

The "problem of the player-character" is central to many discussions of role-playing, so a good place to begin may be with an act of reflecting upon the character one plays in the game. Here is an excerpt from Sam Lipsyte's 2010 *New Yorker* short story "The Dungeon Master," about a group of misfit teenage *D&D* players. The narrator is thinking about his character, having returned home after an afternoon's session of play.

> Today my ranger nearly got the snippo. A giant warthog jumped him in the woods. Is there even a warthog in the game manual? My ranger – his name is Valium, just to tease Marco – cut the beast down, but lost a lot of hit points. Even now, I can picture him bent over a brook, cupping water onto his wounds. Later, he rests in the shade of an oak. The warthog crackles on a spit.[15]

There is a lot going on in this excerpt! There is a distance between player and character – "my ranger," the narrator says, not "I" or "me" – and the character is clearly a construct of the game, having had his "hit points" reduced by a beast that may or may not have come from the official game manual. And yet these game-mechanical elements take on a diegetic (fictional) reality: the narrator understands the lost hit points to be wounds, the damage-dealing antagonist to be a meaty food source – the spoils of victory. And the euphemism "the snippo" for the character's avoided in-game death, taken up from an earlier use in the story, highlights the concern with (character) mortality that is a theme of Lipsyte's story and a feature of role-playing itself.

But what is important for our purposes is the act of player visualization that Lipsyte describes here so skillfully. In a moment outside the play of the game itself, the player reflects upon the character, and imagines him recovering from his battle and quietly enjoying his triumph, safe for the moment. It is that moment of visualization that some players regard as the essence of immersion. It may, however, be hard to achieve, as is suggested by a post on an online discussion forum about tabletop RPGs:

> I've been making an effort at *visualization* – I've been consciously building a picture in my head. I think to myself "*What could my character see from here?*" I deliberately fill in details – "*Can I see the sky from here?*" I ask the GM for more as I realize there are gaps – "*What is the ground made of here, anyway?*" Results from the first three sessions are good – I've seen more impressive pictures than I've ever seen instinctively. More than that – I've managed the sound of the salt river grinding nearby, damp wind in my face, the feel of weathered tiles under my hand. I've never had that in RPGs before. So far, this has been pretty rewarding – almost magical at times.[16]

The fact that this is presented as an *atypical* approach to play, or at least one that requires some effort, invites us to ask about *typical* modes of play if visualization of in-game events is not that mode. The question of imagination is a tricky one in the phenomenological philosophy of mind.[17] Philosophers argue over the nature of "mental images" associated with visualization – what are people *seeing* when they visualize something, and how are those visualizations related to perception, if at all? More broadly, what if anything unites all of the different senses in which we may be said to "imagine" something: as supposition or speculation, as fantasy or daydream, as hallucination or error, and so forth? Some philosophers want to avoid having to explain the nature of mental images (are they *objects* of consciousness, or *by-products* of it?) by defining imagination as fundamentally an act of *description*, involving the formulation of propositions about things that may be merely absent or entirely unreal. However, these linguistic approaches are not wholly satisfying, because they do not seem to do the phenomenon justice on several levels.

Nonetheless, it's important to recognize that role-playing does in fact have a non-visual dimension that may in fact be more characteristic than the visual one. The question is, is that non-visual element *imaginative*? Is it *immersive*?

Am I My Character? Immersion and Identification

The answer seems to be yes, on both counts. In her book about how tabletop games like *Dungeons & Dragons* create narrative, Jennifer Grouling Cover describes a kind of immersion that seems to hinge upon her identification with her character. She recounts an incident from a game in which she played where a conflict between her character, Whisper, and Whisper's companions led to Whisper fleeing from them, being chased, and finding temporary succor before the inevitable confrontation:

> While Whisper was in the cottage attempting to sleep, as a player, I was temporarily removed from the rest of the Sorpraedor group [i.e., her fellow players]. As I awaited my turn, I wrote the following in my personal blog: "For those that don't play, I can't really explain it to you. But I've had a total adrenaline rush going since about 4:00. The tension, the excitement…all maxed out. It's amazing. And the story. Oh, my god…the story is *so good* [ellipsis and emphasis in original].[18]

What Cover seems to find engaging about the game is the way that her decisions on behalf of her character and those of the other players on behalf of theirs interact to create an engrossing fiction. "The scene involving the conflict between Whisper and

David [another character] was extremely suspenseful because the number of paths [i.e., choices available to the characters] seemed significantly reduced. The relationship between these characters had degenerated to the point where it seemed clear that one of them must go, but not knowing which one or how the conflict would go down was incredibly suspenseful for those involved."[19]

Character identification of this sort seems to rely on a kind of *distance* from the character, rather than an undifferentiated total identity with the character. This relationship seems to fall somewhere between that of the author to his or her protagonist (which is very complicated, as literary critic Mikhail Bakhtin has noted, a combination of proprietary ownership and critical commentary[20]) and that of a person to the social roles her or she enacts in daily life (which sometimes feels like play-acting, as sociologist Erving Goffman has pointed out[21]). As Ethan Gilsdorf notes in his account of fantasy role-playing culture, "we all engage in some form of minor dress-up and role-playing. At a wedding or a cocktail party, on a first date or during a job interview, or when home for the holidays, we all dress the part and adopt another character: Witty or Well-Adjusted, Stockbroker or Salesman, Happy or Perfect. Unless you're not willing to play along and put on a mask, friends will say, 'You're not yourself. What's wrong?' Who, indeed, are you, if you're not you?"[22] This is an insight at which many *D&D* players arrive.

Alea and Immersion: The Role of the Dice

We have barely begun to scratch the surface of a complete phenomenological description of role-playing, but one last point needs to be made before concluding this chapter. Thus far, we have focused on the personal, psychological aspects of immersion in *Dungeons & Dragons*. But the game is social and interactive, and mediated by the forces of chance – what sociologist of play Roger Caillois calls "alea."[23] Here's an account of play that illustrates this idea, taken from an article written by one of the early editors of *Dungeons & Dragons* for the readers of *Psychology Today*. The Dungeon Master has determined that one of the characters in his game, a paladin, has been captured by monsters from outer space and imprisoned in a dark tower on a far-off world.

> The paladin [character] came to in a bare cell.... Dave [the player]...knew he was in big trouble, confronting a fate that is *really* worse than death. "What are you going to do?" I asked.... "I'm going to get down on my knees and pray real hard." It was an entirely appropriate response for the virtuous knight, but it was one I had not anticipated.... I explained that a die roll near 100 was required for an answer to his prayers. With the players holding their breath, Dave threw the polyhedrons: 99! The challenge was now mine..."Poised in the air is a huge angel... [who] seizes you in his arms and flies up and away...The angel gently descends to earth.... 'There. Now keep your nose clean.' He's gone." To my delight the players said, "Wow." I had managed to successfully obey the imperatives of our joint imaginary creation. The dice never lie.[24]

To the Dungeon Master, the player's successful die roll was a challenge. Could he come up with a suitably dramatic but believable act of divine intervention – *deus ex machina*, indeed! – in response to the paladin's prayers? The dice serve as another voice in the game whose input guides the outcome of events, at time oracularly. We know that dice loom large in players' accounts of the game and in their superstitions about play. But this episode shows how rolling the dice operates to create the feeling of a world in motion around the players and their characters, a "joint imaginary creation" rather than the sole vision of one person or another.

For Tyros and Grognards

In this brief overview of the phenomenology of *Dungeons & Dragons,* we've seen how visualization is secondary to character identification as a mechanism for immersion, an adjunct rather than a fundamental aspect. We've suggested that character identification operates in the space between the player and the character, and noted that the social and interactive qualities of *Dungeons & Dragons* are enhanced by the role that the dice play in allowing the game-world to "speak" for itself at the table. A complete phenomenology of role-playing would delve further into all of these issues, and could conceivably help phenomenological philosophers make some headway toward understanding imagination phenomenologically! More important for our purposes, however, is that a phenomenology of *Dungeons & Dragons* may help tyros figure out the game, and grognards appreciate its depths.

Notes

1. John Tarnowski, *Dungeons and Dragons and Philosophy* (2012). Available at http://www.therpgsite.com/showthread.php?t=22622. Accessed Nov. 28, 2012.
2. Sephka, *Somebody Explain Dungeons and Dragons To Me* (2003). Available at http://www.head-fi.org/t/48636/someone-explain-dungeons-and-dragons-to-me. Accessed Nov. 28, 2012.
3. Kendall Walton, *Mimesis as Make-Believe: On the Foundations of the Representational Arts* (Cambridge, MA: Harvard University Press, 1990).
4. Henry Jenkins, *Textual Poachers: Television Fans and Participatory Culture* (New York: Routledge, 1992), and *Fans, Bloggers, and Gamers: Exploring Participatory Culture* (New York: New York University Press, 2006).
5. Evan Torner and William J. White. *Immersive Gameplay: Essays on Participatory Media and Role-playing* (Jefferson, NC: McFarland, 2012), p. 3.
6. Mihalyi Csikszentmihalyi, *Flow: The Psychology of Optimal Experience*, 1st edn. (New York: Harper & Row, 1990).
7. William J. White, J. Tuomas Harviainen, and Emily Care Boss. "Role-Playing Communities, Cultures of Play, and the Discourse of Immersion," in Evan Torner and William J. White, eds., *Immersive Gameplay: Essays on Participatory Media and Role-Playing* (Jefferson, NC: McFarland, 2012), pp. 71–86.

8. Janet Horowitz Murray, *Hamlet on the Holodeck: The Future of Narrative in Cyberspace* (New York: Free Press, 1997), p. 98.

9. Katie Salen and Eric Zimmerman, *Rules of Play: Game Design Fundamentals* (Cambridge, MA: MIT Press, 2004), p. 453.

10. David Woodruff Smith, "Phenomenology," in *Stanford Encyclopedia of Philosophy* (Stanford, CA: Stanford University Press, 2008).

11. Maurice Merleau-Ponty, "What Is Phenomenology?", in Ted Toadvine and Leonard Lawlor, eds., *The Merleau-Ponty Reader* (Evanston, IL: Northwestern University Press, 2007), p. 55.

12. Jean-Paul Sartre, *Imagination* (Ann Arbor: University of Michigan Press, 1962), pp. 158–159 n. 4.

13. Ibid., p. 128.

14. Stan Lester, "An Introduction to Phenomenological Research" (1999). Available at http://www.sld.demon.co.uk/resmethy.pdf. Accessed Nov. 3, 2012.

15. Sam Lipsyte, "The Dungeon Master," *New Yorker*, Oct. 4, 2010, p. 88.

16. R. Alexander, "Skills for You-Are-There Immersion," in *Story Games: Tabletop Roleplaying 2.0*. Available at http://www.story-games.com/forums/discussion/17472/skills-for-you-are-there-immersion. Accessed Nov. 4, 2012.

17. Lilly-Marlene Russow, "Some Recent Work on Imagination," *American Philosophical Quarterly* 15 (1978), pp. 57–66.

18. Jennifer Grouling Cover, *The Creation of Narrative in Tabletop Role-Playing Games* (Jefferson, NC: McFarland, 2010), p. 106.

19. Ibid., p. 110.

20. M.M. Bakhtin, "Author and Hero in Aesthetic Activity," in Michael Holquist and Vadim Liapunov, eds., *Art and Answerability: Early Philosophical Essays* (Austin: University of Texas Press, 1990), pp. 4–256.

21. Erving Goffman, *Interaction Ritual: Essays in Dace-to-Face Behavior* (Chicago: Aldine, 1967), and *Strategic Interaction* (Philadelphia: University of Pennsylvania Press, 1969).

22. Ethan Gilsdorf, *Fantasy Freaks and Gaming Geeks* (Guilford, CT: Lyons Press, 2009), p. 59.

23. Roger Caillois, *Man, Play, and Games*, trans. Meyer Barash (Urbana: University of Illinois Press, 2001).

24. John Eric Holmes, "Confessions of a Dungeon Master," *Psychology Today* (Nov. 1980), pp. 84–94.

Part III
CRAFTING WORLDS

Imagination and Creation
The Morality of Fiction in
Dungeons & Dragons

Robert A. Delfino and Jerome C. Hillock

What could be more creative than playing a game of *Dungeons & Dragons*? This first among all tabletop role-playing games employs our imagination in the enjoyment of its fictional worlds. Even better, players actively take on the role of characters in these worlds and collaborate with the Dungeon Master (DM) in shaping the storyline of the game. This adds dimensions to playing *D&D* that our experiences of playing other tabletop games lack.

It's these very features of the game that give it some interesting moral features as well. Both the DM and the players have to make important choices when sitting down at the table. By helping to give life to a fictional world, a DM takes a stand on who the good guys and bad guys are. Heck, entire species of creatures are deemed evil, like orcs or goblins. Similarly, those who play characters have to make important choices about what their characters do. When a player decides that his character is a worthless wretch – in *D&D* terms, the character would be of some or other evil alignment – he'll have his character commit all sorts of heinous acts within

Dungeons & Dragons and Philosophy: Read and Gain Advantage on All Wisdom Checks, First Edition. Edited by Christopher Robichaud.
© 2014 John Wiley & Sons, Inc. Published 2014 by John Wiley & Sons, Inc.

the fictional world of the game that he would never think of doing outside it. (Let's hope!)

This raises an important philosophical question. Can there be anything morally problematic with the fictional worlds we create or the imaginary characters we play in them? Brandon Cooke argues that there is "absolutely nothing wrong with role-playing a thoroughly evil villain."[1] Others are less sanguine, criticizing the fictional worlds common to so much of *D&D*. For example, William Schnoebelen argues that the fictional world of magic and dark forces that we typically find in *D&D* is inherently dangerous and, therefore, the game should never be played.[2] As we shall argue later on, we think this view is dead wrong. But in order to cast a light spell on the matter, we first need to grab one of those dusty tomes in our wizard's library and discuss some metaphysics, a branch of philosophy that deals with some of the deepest features of the world. So grab some rations, supplies, and whatever else you need, and let's delve in.

The Traditionalists (aka the "Lawful Good")

Plato (c.429–c.347 BCE), in the ancient world, Thomas Aquinas (1225–74), in the medieval world, and J.R.R. Tolkien (1892–1973), in the contemporary world, all count as traditionalists in what will be our use of the term. What unites them is that they all hold that everything in universe has a purpose. In metaphysics this is known as a teleological view. It comes from the ancient Greek word *telos*, meaning purpose or end. The end of a thing is the purpose for which it was made. For example, the end of a shield is to protect you in battle against attacks. A shield that is weak and breaks often when hit by a mace or a sword is a bad shield. According to the teleological view, a thing is good only to the extent that it fulfills the end for which it was made.

The teleological view raises some interesting philosophical questions. If everything has a purpose, what is the purpose of human beings? And what is the ultimate source responsible for purpose in the universe? The traditionalists agree, more or less, in their answers to these questions. Concerning the source of the teleology, they all say it is some kind of Divine Intellect that transcends the physical world. And this intellect, in *D&D* terms, is Lawful Good. For Plato, it seems to be the *Demiurgos* (Divine Craftsman), though some scholars disagree. For Aquinas and Tolkien, both Christians, the source of the teleology is God. And spending existence in some kind of afterlife with the Divine is their answer to the second question concerning the purpose, or ultimate destiny, of human beings. For only such a life, according to the traditionalists, could completely satisfy our unlimited desires for knowledge and happiness.

By holding that human nature finds its purpose and fulfillment in the Divine, which is eternal and transcendent, the traditionalists provide us with a clear way of measuring whether something in our earthly life is good or evil. To the extent that something harms our nature or hinders us from obtaining our ultimate purpose, it is evil. And to the extent that something perfects our nature or helps us to obtain our ultimate purpose, it is good. Naturally, this understanding applies to art and to *D&D*, since it is a kind of art. A *D&D* game that helps us to become better persons, and thereby helps us to obtain our ultimate goal, is a good game. But it is possible that a *D&D* game might, in some circumstances, make us worse persons and thereby hinder our ability to obtain our ultimate goal, which would make that particular game bad for us.

Let's examine the traditionalists' arguments why *D&D* is good for us first, and then we'll discuss the cases where it could be bad for us.

D&D Rules!

Much that Plato says about the nature and purpose of art can be used to defend *D&D*. For Plato, the purpose of art is to educate – to lead the highest part of the soul to love and rejoice in the existence of what is most good.[3] As such, good art has a beneficial impact on a person's moral character and helps a person to seek the higher things. For this reason, Plato would certainly approve of a *D&D* game where the players learn important truths about the soul, for example, or about moral virtues, such as justice. Indeed, Plato himself used myths in his own philosophical writings to help awaken the human mind to important truths.[4]

It is true that Plato banned poetry from his utopian republic, because it can spread falsehoods about reality.[5] However, we don't think such an argument could ever be applied to *D&D*. Except, perhaps, in some rare cases, those who play *D&D* are quite aware that the world of *D&D* is a fictional world and therefore there is little danger in the game spreading falsehoods about the real world. In this we agree with Cooke, who has argued: "None of the game materials assert that any of the truths of the game world are true in the actual world. So if, somehow, someone did manage to acquire false beliefs about the real world from the game, the epistemic fault lies with that person, not the game."[6]

We think that Plato's student, Aristotle (384–322 BCE), has a better view of poetry, and by extension fantasy role-playing. Aristotle argued that poetry was more philosophical than history for two reasons.[7] First, it can be about things that have not happened in history. In that sense it is very creative, allowing us to explore in the labyrinth of our mind all sorts of philosophically interesting scenarios. Second, poetry can be used to express important universal themes and truths, such as the importance of courage and sacrifice. Imagining how we would act in these scenarios and reflecting on these themes can help us to grow intellectually and morally as persons. Similarly, the storyline of a good *D&D* game can help us to think creatively and philosophically, enhancing our intellectual and moral lives.

Turning to the philosophy of the great medieval cleric Aquinas, we find an even stronger justification for playing *D&D*. For Aquinas, the human creation of art, when done properly, is an imitation of God's creative activity and is, therefore, good. Indeed, as Armand Maurer has commented,

Aquinas held that God specifically intended for humans to be co-creators with him:

> Having supplied mankind with intelligence, God left nature in his keeping, to guard it, cultivate it, make it fruitful and fill it with his offspring. The art of man was meant to serve nature...to continue its creative activity. Man, by his art, was intended to be a co-creator with God, continuing nature's creative activity in the world.[8]

Of course, as alluded to above, Aquinas argues that art should be used in a morally responsible way. Had he played *D&D*, Aquinas never would have played a chaotic evil character. And we're pretty sure if Aquinas were a DM, his campaigns would have been about the triumph of good over evil. But let's assume, for the sake of argument, that some people will play *D&D* in a morally objectionable way. Would that be enough, for Aquinas, to justify banning the game? We think not. Aquinas addressed a very similar question about art when he said "But in the case of an art the products of which may be employed by man either for a good or for an evil use, such as swords, arrows, and the like, the practice of such an art is not sinful."[9]

Concerning the role of the imagination in the creation of art, Aquinas only speaks briefly. However, this theme was taken up and developed more fully by Tolkien. Aquinas and Tolkien agree that humans are in the image of God because of their ability to know and make free choices. But Tolkien, more than Aquinas, develops the idea that our desire to create imaginary worlds is another way in which we reflect the image of God. Tolkien uses the word "sub-creation" to distinguish the human creation of imaginary worlds from God's creative activity.

For Tolkien, the sub-creation of imaginary worlds is a natural activity for human beings. More than this, it is a human right as it was intended by God that we should participate, in our own way, in God's creative activity. As Tolkien explains: "Fantasy remains a human right: we make in our measure and in our derivative mode, because we are made: and not only made, but made in the image and likeness of a Maker."[10] Although, obviously, Tolkien did not discuss *D&D*, we think his arguments above can be used to defend the playing of *D&D*, as long as the game is used in a morally responsible manner. It's not difficult for us to imagine Tolkien acting as a DM to his sons, taking them on grand adventures designed to teach them the importance of love and justice.

By now it should be clear that we find, among the traditionalists, strong arguments that support the playing of *D&D* provided it is done properly. And the irony for Christian critics of *D&D*, such as Schnoebelen, is that the philosophical and theological arguments of Christian traditionalists, such as Aquinas and Tolkien, provide some of the strongest arguments in favor of *D&D* role-playing. However, to be fair, these same arguments can be used to argue that a particular *D&D* game, under certain circumstances, can be bad. Let's examine some of those cases.

Lost in the Labyrinth?

We believe the vast majority of *D&D* games are morally acceptable. However, there are two kinds of potential problems that can arise which merit our attention.

The first potential problem is escapism, which comes in two varieties. The first variety we think is very rare. It would be the case of the person who over time blurs the distinction between the fictional world they play in and the real world they live in. Clearly, such delusional behavior would only be possible where there is already a serious underlying psychological problem or pre-condition. Thus the fault, in this case, lies within the person and not the game. We believe this is so rare as not to warrant further comment.

The second variety of escapism is more common and much less severe, but still problematic. It occurs when a person, understanding that the fictional world of the *D&D* game is not real, still prefers to spend large amounts of time playing in or working on the game and thereby neglects the duties and responsibilities they have in the real world. This is probably more common with fantasy videogames, which we (and we are sure many others!) have sometimes played to excess. How many of you have neglected school work (or other work) to continue playing a videogame? It can also happen with *D&D*. Still, again, the fault here lies with the person, who is irresponsible, and not with the game.

The second potential problem involves the game's potential effect on our moral character in real life. The traditionalists generally understand moral character as a set of dispositions we have, which incline us to behave in certain ways in life. Following Aristotle, good dispositions, such as courage and justice, are called virtues. Bad dispositions, such as cowardice and injustice, are called vices. According to Aristotle, virtues and vices are obtained through habitual action – that is, we obtain them when we do the same kind of action over and over.[11] So, for example, the more you tell the truth in life the more you feel inclined to tell the truth. Eventually, you acquire a stable disposition to tell the truth, and at that point you possess the virtue of honesty.

But consider the following. What if, during a long campaign, you play a thoroughly evil villain who lies very frequently in the game? Is it not possible that over time you might find yourself becoming more comfortable with telling lies in the real world? Or suppose, during a long campaign, you play an assassin who routinely murders in grotesque ways. Is it not possible that this might desensitize you to violence, to some degree, in real life? We think that a player should be responsible enough to stop playing an evil character if there is recognition that his or her moral character in the real world is being affected. But, of course, we also think it is possible for very mature and responsible players to play evil characters, within certain limits, with no ill effects.

Things can also go wrong if the DM acts irresponsibly. Indeed, as the creator of the storyline in the fictional world, the DM bears great responsibility as to what the moral climate of the game will be. The DM can choose to reward virtue and punish vice, or to do the opposite. Things can go too far if, for example, the DM encourages a character to act in increasingly sadistic ways, or if a DM lavishly rewards a character, say, for raping his victims prior to killing them. As some psychologists have argued, too much moral inversion (treating what is normally considered evil as good) in a game can have bad effects on the mind.[12] Although the science is not settled on this issue, at the very least, these potential problems highlight the importance of the moral dimension of fiction in *D&D*, the need for players and the DM to be responsible, and the need for parents to oversee the game from time to time when the participants are young. We certainly wouldn't want our sons reveling in their roles as evil fighters, who rape, murder, and pillage, in a year-long campaign.

At least, that is what the traditionalists would argue. As we mentioned earlier, there is another philosophical school of thought on these matters called the postmodernists. Let's explore what they have to say.

The Postmodernists (aka "Chaotic" and beyond Good and Evil...)

"Postmodernists" refers loosely to a group of philosophers and thinkers who question, if not outright reject, the core tenets of the traditionalists. Chief among them, for our purposes, is the Dark Wizard himself, the philosopher Friedrich Nietzsche (1844–1900). Nietzsche rejects both the teleology of the traditionalists and the Divinity behind it. Traditionalists put limits on the use of imagination and creativity; they must not harm our nature or hinder our purpose. By contrast, Nietzsche thinks there should be no limits on human imagination or the human will. In this he is the polar opposite of the traditionalists, as Richard Kearney explains:

> [For Nietzsche, the] creative imagination is indeed foundation-less, a free-floating nothingness, pure will and desire. But therein lies its virtue. Therein reposes the incontrovertible challenge of modern man to exist without alibi or reprieve, without any

recourse to higher values. Imagination, for Nietzsche, is the demand to 'live dangerously'...Only when the last lingering belief in a transcendent deity disappears can creative imagination come into its own. Then at last man is free to invent the project of the super-man (*Uebermensch*): the great individual who dares to make his arbitrary existence into a work of art. The productive imagination thereby assumes its existential vocation as a will to power in a meaningless world. This unmitigated voluntarism takes, in Nietzsche, the form of a "transvaluation of values" which dismantles the traditional notions of truth and morality.[13]

What dark magic is this? In declaring the collapse of traditional notions of truth and morality, Nietzsche seems to be embracing anti-realism, the view that traditional philosophical notions of good and evil, truth and falsehood, are nothing more than the constructions of human beings. Indeed, Nietzsche himself says as much in *The Will to Power*: "'Truth' is therefore not something there, that might be found or discovered – but something that must be created.... It is a word for the 'will to power.'"[14]

But if moral truths are merely arbitrary creations of human beings, then we have no objective basis on which to judge them. It becomes difficult to see how we could criticize any behavior in the real world, let alone behavior in a fictional world. In fact, Nietzsche appears to be blurring the traditional distinction between fictional worlds and the real world. Dark magic, indeed!

A New Quest

So which side is correct – the traditionalists or the postmodernists? Let's review what we have argued up till this point. If the traditionalists have the correct metaphysics about the real world, then it follows that *D&D* is good, but that care must be taken to make sure the game does not become morally objectionable. However, if the postmodernists have the correct understanding of things then "anything goes" when playing a character in the fictional world of *D&D*, or when a DM designs an imaginary world. Although we argued for these conclusions, we did not spend time giving arguments as to which metaphysical understanding of the real world is the correct one. That would require much more space than we have available to us here.

To resolve that issue requires you, the reader, to take up a new quest – the quest of philosophy. The goal of philosophy is to find the correct answers to these kinds of metaphysical questions, and, of course, other important questions. Philosophy is not something someone else can do for you; it should not be accepted on faith. You have to investigate the topic, gather the evidence, and weigh the arguments. In the process you will grow in experience and wisdom – just as in *D&D* acquiring experience points and leveling up is something only you can do for yourself. So, we encourage you to take up this new quest. Of course, the choice whether to begin this adventure is yours alone.

Acknowledgments

We would like to thank William Irwin, Christopher Robichaud, Tony Spanakos, William Byrne, and David Kaspar, for their helpful comments and suggestions on this paper.

Notes

1. Brandon Cooke, "It's Okay to Be Evil in Your Head," in *Dungeons and Dragons and Philosophy: Raiding the Temple of Wisdom* (Chicago: Open Court, 2012), p. 76.
2. William Schnoebelen, "Should a Christian Play Dungeons & Dragons?" Available at http://www.chick.com/articles/frpg.asp. Accessed March 24, 2014.
3. Plato, *Republic*, Book VII, 532, and *Symposium*, 210–212.
4. Consider, as just two examples, the myth of Er in Book X of *Republic*, 614–621, and the myth of the chariot in *Phaedrus*, 246–254.

5. Plato, *Republic*, Book X, 607–608. Plato does seem to allow some poetry in his ideal society, for example, poetry that praises good men and the gods.

6. Cooke, "It's Okay to Be Evil in Your Head," p. 77.

7. Aristotle, *Poetics*, ch. 9.

8. Armand A. Maurer, *About Beauty: A Thomistic Interpretation* (Houston: Center for Thomistic Studies, 1983), p. 84.

9. Thomas Aquinas, *Summa Theologiae*, II-II, 169, a. 2, reply to objection 4.

10. J.R.R. Tolkien, "On Fairy-Stories," in Verlyn Flieger and Douglas A. Anderson, eds., *Tolkien On Fairy-Stories* (London: HarperCollins, 2008), pp. 65–66.

11. Aristotle, *Nicomachean Ethics*, Book II, ch. 1.

12. Leonard Sax, *Why Gender Matters: What Parents and Teachers Need to Know about the Emerging Science of Sex Differences* (New York: Harmony, 2006), p. 71.

13. Richard Kearney, *The Wake of Imagination: Toward a Postmodern Culture* (Minneapolis: University of Minnesota Press, 1988), p. 211.

14. Friedrich Nietzsche, *The Will to Power*, trans. Walter Kaufmann and R.J. Hollingdale (New York: Vintage Books, 1968), para. 552 (p. 298).

Dungeonmastery as Soulcraft

Ben Dyer

My friend is adamant: second edition *Dungeons & Dragons* is the best edition of the game. I'm rather agnostic about editions, but when I asked him why he wasn't, his answer was interesting. "It's because they published more material for second edition than for any other edition before or since." I don't know if that's true, but it sounds plausible. Second edition was when something important about *D&D* changed. Monte Cook summarized it when he said that "worldbuilding became more important than adventure design."[1] Where earlier editions published adventures that delved into dark and dangerous dungeons, second edition publications filled in worlds around them as *D&D* gained popularity.

It's no accident that *D&D* grew in this way. Fantasy role-playing drew from a narrower collection of literary sources than are available today, and though the shade of Gary Gygax may haunt me for it, I'm going to suggest in spite of him that the most important of these were the works of J.R.R. Tolkien. But not for the reason you may suspect. It's true that elves, dwarves, wizards, dragons, magic, and many other characteristic features of modern fantasy were given their contemporary forms in Tolkien's work. Gygax and Dave Arneson drew from the work of many authors,

Dungeons & Dragons and Philosophy: Read and Gain Advantage on All Wisdom Checks, First Edition. Edited by Christopher Robichaud.
© 2014 John Wiley & Sons, Inc. Published 2014 by John Wiley & Sons, Inc.

including Michael Moorcock, Robert E. Howard, Jack Vance, and others. These sources, together with history and mythology, were significant in the development of *D&D*. But it was Tolkien's commitment to building a coherent secondary world that was his greatest influence on aspiring Dungeon Masters, and as *D&D* grew, so too did the tools necessary to build the world beyond the dungeon. Dungeon Masters may or may not make use of familiar fantasy elements whose beginnings lay with Tolkien, but they must always put their players in a world. Dark Sun, Eberron, and the Planar City of Sigil little resemble the history, languages, lands, peoples, and places of Middle Earth, but they follow Tolkien's practice of creating a world in which all these elements are meant to fit together. Many of us have nigh-encyclopedic knowledge of Tolkien's world. (Some of us even speak the language.) But have you ever learned what Tolkien had to say about world-building?

The Essence of Fantasy

In 1939 Tolkien delivered a lecture that was later published as the essay, "On Fairy-Stories." In it, he describes the essential character of fantasy. To get at that essence, Tolkien first sets aside features that are incidental. Although we first learn these stories in childhood, fantasy stories are not simply children's stories. Although they frequently feature intelligent talking animals, they are not what Tolkien called, "beast-fables." Although they often include great journeys, fantasy stories are not simply travel narratives. All of these kinds of stories have been told without reference to anything "fantastic." *Planet of the Apes* and *Star Trek* are both fascinating, but they aren't fantasy as Tolkien understands it.

No, fantasy is something that happens when we are taken out of this world and into another by a special kind of enchantment: the adjective. Relative to the invention of the adjective, Tolkien writes, "no spell or incantation in Faerie is more potent." What makes adjectives so special? Tolkien explains that:

When we can take green from grass, blue from heaven, and red
from blood, we have already an enchanter's power…we may put
a deadly green upon a man's face and produce a horror; we may
make the rare and terrible blue moon to shine; or we may cause
woods to spring with silver leaves and rams to wear fleeces of
gold, and put hot fire into the belly of the cold worm.[2]

The first part of fantasy, then, is the human capacity to separate the
qualities of things (redness, sharpness, hotness, etc.) from the things
in which they appear, and to imagine them in other things that do
not have them. However, imaginative reconstruction is not itself
fantasy. For the capacity to imaginatively imbue the cold worm's
belly with hot fire (or acid, or frost, or other chromatic dragon
powers) is not by itself sufficient to bring us away into Faerie or
Feywild. These realms require more than imagination. They require
what Tolkien calls "the inner consistency of reality."

Inner consistency allows a "secondary world" to command
"secondary belief," and us to enter in by the enchantment of the
storyteller's craft. This consistency in craft is well known to Tolkien's
readers, and it is the Everest for many a DM because it is difficult to
achieve. After all, what would it be like to live in a world of long-lived
elder races? What is commerce and technology like in a world
where magic is plentiful? And what are the ecological requirements
of a huge dragon living in the depths of a dungeon whose only
entrance is sized for ordinary human passage? When inner consistency fails, we are jarred out of that other world. However, when we
do achieve it, "Faerie begins; Man becomes a sub-creator."[3]

This idea of sub-creation is fundamental to Tolkien's conception of fantasy, but it's a strange compound term. Typically
we now describe writers as "creators" or "creative," not "sub-
creators" or "sub-creative," but Tolkien's terms do not demean
his craft. As a sincere Catholic, Tolkien believed that the
creative impulse was not itself original to the human condition,
but was an inheritance of the Divine image present in all human
beings. To be made in the image of God was to be made in the
resemblance of a creator, and therefore to inherit the creative
impulse. As Tolkien says, "we make in our measure and in our

derivative mode, because we are made: and not only made, but made in the image and likeness of a Maker."[4] So, we are sub-creators because we imitate our own creator, and because we create within an existing created order. Imagining a deadly green upon a man's face is not, as it happens, quite the same thing as imagining green itself as an original creative act. One is well within our creative powers, the other is not.

Sub-creation then is the essence of fantasy for Tolkien. It is our inheritance as special creatures of God endowed with his image, and it is made possible by our care in crafting a secondary world with inner consistency sufficient to bring our readers or players into it. This is surely a great power, and Tolkien reminds us that though it can be put to evil uses, "of what human thing in this fallen world is that not true? Men have conceived not only of elves, but they have imagined gods, and worshipped them, even worshipped those most deformed by their authors' own evil."[5] He continues by reminding us that humans have even worshipped their own materials by offering human sacrifice to idols of money, science, and social and economic theories. Tolkien allows that our fantasy worlds may be filled with evil and darkness, but he reminds us that it was we who made them so. It is not essential to being a fantastic world that it be dark and evil as well. In fact, Tolkien's fellow-Catholic and near-contemporary G.K. Chesterton reminds us that the opposite is more typically true.

The Magic of Morality

"The Ethics of Elfland" is the aptly titled fourth chapter of G.K. Chesterton's book *Orthodoxy*, and in it he writes: "My first and last philosophy, that which I believe with unbroken certainty, I learnt in the nursery."[6] Fairy tales seemed to Chesterton "entirely reasonable things" because they respect principles of necessity (for example, that $2 + 2 = 4$, or that sons are younger than their fathers), but recognize that all else could possibly have been different. This latter possibility is what philosophers call "contingency." Notice that Tolkien's enchanting adjectives are about the contingent things in the world, while his requirement of internal consistency is about respecting matters of necessity. What Chesterton adds is the insight that fairy tales are not just descriptions of alternate flora, fauna, peoples, and places. That much might be achieved by stories of alternate history or alien worlds. No, fairy tales contain something more than that. They contain magic.

Chesterton approaches this quality of faerie by introducing his readers to what he calls, the "Doctrine of Conditional Joy." In fairy tales, all joy and happiness, all ruin and suffering, turn on an "if." He explains that:

> In the fairy tale an incomprehensible happiness rests upon an incomprehensible condition. A box is opened, and all evils fly out. A word is forgotten, and cities perish. A lamp is lit, and love flies away. A flower is plucked, and human lives are forfeited. An apple is eaten, and the hope of God is gone.[7]

That first sentence is where we learn about what magic is. The incomprehensible condition is a hidden connection between apparently unrelated things. Why does forgetting a word destroy a city? Why does lighting a lamp extinguish love? These things are unrelated in our world, but in fairy tales things turned out differently. Although the connection is mysterious, it is no less lawful and binding than the laws that govern the rest of the universe. That's what magic is, the hidden connection between apparently unrelated things.

This conception of magic comes to us from the Renaissance, when magic was regarded as a branch of natural philosophy. Renaissance natural philosophers sought to manipulate "occult qualities" that were naturally present in the world. Although modern usage has associated the word "occult" with supernatural phenomena, the original Latin definition simply means "hidden." Occult qualities then were contrasted against the manifest qualities of things perceived by our five senses. Magnetism was thought to be an occult quality, as was gravity, and any other mysterious correlation between two apparently unrelated things. The Moon, for example, had manifest qualities such as being bright, white, and round, but it was in virtue of some hidden quality that it influenced the tides. Both manifest and occult properties were part of nature, and just as one might manipulate the manifest properties of a thing (its color, shape, temperature, and so on), so too might one manipulate something through its occult properties. If this conception of magic seems familiar, it should. It's the reason wizards require material components to cast spells.

Many *D&D* campaigns treat magic as a kind of alternate science, but in fairy tales there is more to it than that. Chesterton's examples include Pandora's Box and the Garden of Eden, after all. In fairy tales, the incomprehensible conditions of faerie magic are typically moral. Cinderella receives a coach and a wardrobe upgrade, but they come with a curfew. Faerie magic can make men into frogs, but faeries are, Chesterton says, "slaves of duty." The essential fabric of the land of faerie is morally significant because its conditional joy – its magic – is as fundamental to it as are the empirical facts about its winding rivers and ancient groves. In fact, morality is even more fundamental to the fairy tale because, like principles of necessity, fairy tale morality exists here in our world as well. In fairy tales, we learn from Sleeping Beauty how "the human creature was blessed with all birthday gifts, yet cursed with death; and how death may be softened to a sleep."[8] From Cinderella we learn that humility is praiseworthy, from Beauty and the Beast that lovable things must first be loved, and from the Frog Prince that promises must be kept. Accordingly, faerie lands are not simply internally consistent alternate realities. They are certainly that, but they are also magical realms whose hidden principles make joy and happiness conditional on our good behavior.

The Consolation of Fantasy

The notion that fantasy has morality in its DNA may leave some readers squirming and other readers skeptical. Conan, Elric, the Black Company, and nearly the whole of Westeros are quite amoral, but they are clearly within canon of fantasy literature. Are these characters not examples of an adult art form that leaves behind the black and white moralizing of the nursery? Seriously, when was the last time anyone *started* character creation by choosing an alignment? Morality tales are perhaps useful for the moral formation of children, but fantasy has grown up since Tolkien first gave his talk on fairy stories.

Except that it hasn't. Or to be more precise, Tolkien understood fantasy as something already fully grown. Fantasy succeeds when it transports us to an imaginary land, and we escape the grayer parts of our own for a little while. Escapism is frequently described negatively (especially in relation to fantasy role-playing), but Tolkien reminds us that there are nobler escapisms. Beyond the desire to be free of traffic noise or workplace drudgery, there is also the desire to escape injustice, pain, sorrow, and, greater than these, death. This last is the most ancient desire for escape, and it is in that desire that the literary value of fantasy is born. Fairy tales are replete with deathless beings, narrow escapes from certain doom, and the eternal joy implicit in the phrase, "happily ever after."

Tolkien writes that the "consolation of the happy ending" is necessary to the fairy story because its literary function is the opposite of tragedy. This opposition may seem strange to students of literature. Literary scholars typically identify comedy as tragedy's opposite because comedy inverts the structure of tragedy. In a tragedy, a good and noble person (a Danish prince or a Scottish king, say) is brought low as the result of a tragic flaw in their character. Comedy inverts this outcome by exalting a foolish or unworthy person (a sarcastic bachelor who vows never to marry or a worldly gravedigger, say) *in spite of* his or her flaws. Tolkien's insight about how fantasy works is that it functionally resembles tragedy, but that it succeeds as fantasy when it subverts the tragic end without breaking the internal principles of the story. Tragic heroes (and the best player-characters) are noble, flawed, and might be destroyed by choices consistent with their character, except that the story subverts this outcome with the consolation of the happy ending. The opposition to tragedy is not the inversion of the protagonist's nobility but the unexpected consolation of the protagonist's outcome.

Tolkien's term for this consolation is "eucatastrophe," which describes "the good catastrophe, the sudden joyous 'turn'" of the happy ending. *D&D* players know it as the natural twenty (or the villain's critical failure) in the last encounter. Grown readers may feel an urge to dismiss such sudden turns as naive or convenient, but what Tolkien has in mind is neither of those things.

> It is a sudden and miraculous grace: never to be counted on to recur. It does not deny the existence of *dyscatastrophe*, of sorrow and failure ... it denies (in the face of much evidence, if you will) universal final defeat and in so far is *evangelium*, giving a fleeting glimpse of Joy, Joy beyond the walls of the world, poignant as grief.[9]

Eucatastrophe is not a happy ending brought about by contrivance, for that would violate the fantasy world's internal consistency. Nor is eucatastrophe the happy ending made possible by sanitizing the fantasy world of danger or evil, for doing so would undermine the value and poignancy of the sudden turn. In fact, Tolkien sees the literary value of fantasy as dependent on *not* cheating the reader of that value.

> It is the mark of a good fairy-story, of the higher or more complete kind, that however wild its events, however fantastic or terrible the adventures, it can give to child or man that hears it, when the "turn" comes, a catch of the breath, a beat and lifting of the heart, near to (or indeed accompanied by) tears, as keen as that given by any form of literary art, and having a peculiar quality.[10]

Eucatastrophe – the consolation of the fairy tale in its highest or most complete form – is only possible when it actually is a consolation. That is, it is only possible when goodness is requited and evil is thwarted. That Frodo's will is finally broken by the power of the ring at the precipice of Mount Doom is a mark of

Tolkien's commitment to consistency, but it is Gollum's fall that is the story's miraculous grace. Sauron is destroyed at just the moment when his last stroke would have destroyed Gandalf, Aragorn, Gimli, Legolas, Pippin, and the remaining strength of Gondor and Rohan. Suddenly, at the moment when destruction seems most certain, the monstrous army streaming from the Black Gate falls into disarray, and the eagles bear Frodo and Sam away from the destruction of Mount Doom. The sudden turn from tragedy to joy is complete, and *Lord of the Rings* is elevated as a work of literary fantasy for the ages.

Worldbuilding as Moral Expression

Now back to the table. Ancient creation epics are about the formation of the world and the filling of it with creatures who call it home. Similarly, Dungeon Masters create planes, worlds, regions, cities, and dungeons. These are filled with NPCs to aid, complicate, and oppose the characters' journey through them. Running through all of these is magic, which beats at the heart of the world of fantasy. It runs through veins of mithril and lifts monstrous dragons on mighty wings. With each choice, the development of a fantasy world (and subsequent campaign) reveals something about the mind of the DM who creates it. When the DM brings dragons to life with an initiative roll, when he lays empires low with a powerful artifact, or when he ends an age with the death of an arch-lich, he enchants his players with adjectives, and they escape into his world if he has been careful and consistent in thought and description. All this is already well known to most DMs, but less well known is that DMs also communicate their moral assumptions to their players in the nature and action of their world as well.

What does success look like? Under what conditions do people flourish? What is the basis of joy? What is best in life? Okay, granted, most *D&D* players answer that last question with a rote barbaric catechism, but who really thinks the right answer is crushing our enemies, seeing them driven before us, and hearing the lamentation of their women? DMs don't just write the physical parameters of the world, they write its story as well. They turn the wheel of fortune and preside over the fates of their world's inhabitants. What they write tells us something about their moral assumptions. The DM cannot say of the death of a noble character or the final victory of an evil character that he was constrained by the bounds of realism when it was that same DM who established the bounds of the real in the fantasy world in the first place. Remember that fantasy succeeds when it satisfies the desire to escape into a different kind of world, but Chesterton's Doctrine of Conditional Joy and Tolkien's concept of eucatastrophe remind us that, at its heart, fantasy is about satisfying the desire to escape sorrow, injustice, and death, not the cultural or technological trappings of everyday life. In a very real sense then, to the extent that DMs build and campaign in fantasy worlds, their sub-creation expresses moral assumptions according to the principles at work (hidden or manifest) in those worlds.

Players express moral assumptions on the scale of the individual character as well. When players build characters, they imagine a being with a particular moral outlook (an alignment). Motivated and directed by that alignment, that character then makes morally significant decisions during the course of the game. Players expect that on some level their characters are worthy of success, whether or not they succeed in looting the room or beating the villain in the final encounter. So, building a character is in essence expressing assumptions about what is worth rewarding in life. This does not imply that only paladins are permissible character choices. Robin Hood is certainly not overly obsessed with obedience to law, and within certain constraints, heist movies and thief fiction (for example, Scott Lynch's excellent *Gentleman Bastards* books) present us with credible heroes who exhibit personal virtues, if not wholly social ones. Imagine for contrast the player who felt the poignant joy Tolkien describes above (the catching breath, the beating heart, and the keen tears of joy) as his evil-aligned character burned down an orphanage and tortured small children for the sheer (and literal) hell of it. Such actions would make the character morally repugnant, and because of what a character is, they would make the player who idealizes them so as well.

Thus, at the table, players and DM together sub-create worlds and the characters who inhabit them. They express their moral assumptions to one another in the choices that both players and DM make at the table. Justice, generosity, compassion, loyalty, hatred, greed, selfishness, and the whole panoply of human experience are woven into the story (and the deep structure) of any fantasy world. Whatever great deeds the characters accomplish and whatever rewards or punishments follow from the contingent principles (manifest or hidden) that govern the world consistently, the sub-creative choices made by the gaming group as an ensemble is as formative to their shared world – to their fantasy ideal – as any song of creation.

Missed Opportunities

With all this talk of moral expression and sub-creation at the game table, there is a footnote in the history of *D&D* that should not go unmarked. In the 1980s, a little before *D&D*'s second edition went into development, media reports linking *D&D* to teen suicides began emerging. *60 Minutes* ran a segment about it as concern grew among parents and educators. Religious groups became concerned that children were being exposed to (or worse, were participating in) witchcraft and Satanism. There was a kind of irony in this because some of *D&D*'s most influential creators – Gary Gygax and Tracy Hickman – were themselves people of faith. Perhaps the high water mark of the "*D&D* scare" among the faithful was the "Dark Dungeons" tract published by Jack Chick, which depicted an inevitable descent into Satanism and suicide for innocent souls ensnared by *D&D*.

Thankfully, people eventually noticed that millions of kids were playing *D&D* without descending into Satanism and suicide, and studies showed that suicide rates among gamers were actually lower than the national average. Panic among parents and educators eventually subsided, and *Dungeons & Dragons* joined comic books, heavy metal, and Socrates in the list of those unjustly accused of corrupting the young.

This last association with Socrates (and philosophy by extension) is perhaps the most informative parallel, because philosophy furnishes a set of tools with which to think about the way the world is, and the way it might be. It interrogates our moral intuitions and offers us the same question we answer in our sub-created characters. How is it best to live, and what kind of life is worthy of success? Philosophy helps us answer these questions in our world, and in any world to which we might escape as sub-creators. We may have good or bad answers in any of these. Thus, it is an unfortunate irony that the parents and educators so deeply concerned over the influence of *Dungeons & Dragons* failed to see that its sources in fairy tales merely furnished them with an alternative presentation for materials that had been used for centuries to teach morality to children. Perhaps we can forgive them to the extent that fairy tales do not typically invite us to play in them. The invitation to do so is a heady liberty after all, and liberties imply corollary responsibilities that children could be unprepared for if left to their own devices. Still, to the extent that *Dungeons & Dragons* allows us to build worlds and collectively escape into them for a little while, Tolkien and Chesterton remind us that if these are fantasy worlds in the truest sense, we are likely to return from them better than when we left.

Notes

1. Monte Cook, *Uniting the Editions: Part 1* (Jan. 30, 2012). Available at http://www.wizards.com/dnd/Article.aspx?x=dnd/4ll/20120130. Accessed Jan. 21, 2014.
2. J.R.R. Tolkien, "On Fairy-Stories," in *A Tolkien Miscellany* (New York: Houghton Mifflin, 2002), pp. 108–109.
3. Ibid., p. 109.
4. Ibid., p. 128.

5. Ibid.
6. G.K. Chesterton, "The Ethics of Elfland," in *Orthodoxy* (1st pub. 1908; New York: Doubleday, 2001), p. 46.
7. Ibid., p. 53.
8. Ibid., p. 47.
9. Tolkien, "On Fairy-Stories," pp. 135–136.
10. Ibid., p. 136.

Part IV

FORAY INTO THE FORGOTTEN REALMS AND DRAGONLANCE

9

Menzoberranzan
A Perfect Unjust State

Matt Hummel

We can all probably agree that Menzoberranzan is very near the bottom on the list of must-visit fantasy realms (worse than Mordor and the ninth circle of hell combined!). Menzoberranzan is the primary setting of R.A. Salvatore's *Homeland* in the Dark Elf trilogy and home of the evil race of dark elves known as drow.[1] Even the prospect of visiting Menzoberranzan as one of its natives, therefore lessening the chance of immediate demise, does not improve the attraction of the most wicked city in the Underdark because drow life operates on one rule: "You may do whatever you can get away with…that is all that matters."[2] That rule creates a very hostile situation where one can never turn one's back on anybody, not even close relatives (just ask the former first son of House Do'Urden, Nalfein, viciously and literally backstabbed by his power-thirsty brother Dinin).

But so what, right? Doing whatever you can get away with seems to have an upside so long as you are VERY good at getting away with things. Perfect crimes are silently applauded in Menzoberranzan – a House that completely annihilates another House of higher rank without a trace thus improves its rank, no questions asked. In a city where rank means everything from greater wealth to favor from an evil deity, being bad can result

Dungeons & Dragons and Philosophy: Read and Gain Advantage on All Wisdom Checks, First Edition. Edited by Christopher Robichaud.
© 2014 John Wiley & Sons, Inc. Published 2014 by John Wiley & Sons, Inc.

in a pretty sweet deal. It's only when someone gets caught that severe punishment is doled out, and we're talking utterly cruel and unusual here (a dozen piercing crossbow arrows, three bolts of lightning, and then savagely eaten by a hideous monster from some horrible plane of existence ... for starters).[3] What does this say about justice or the importance of being a moral person? If being bad brings about a better life so long as no one knows it was you, why be good? To answer this question we'll move from Menzoberranzan to Athens in order to consult Plato (c.429–c.347 BCE).

The Myth of Gyges

Plato's *Republic* features characters at a feast discussing the topic of justice (not all dinner conversations can be about how much the highest-ranked House Baenre sucks).[4] Glaucon, one of the conversation partners, decides to play devil's advocate, putting forth the idea that justice is one of those pesky things we have to deal with to live in a peaceful society, arguing that if there were a way around it, no one would be just or moral.[5] Glaucon declares, "wherever anyone thinks he can be safely unjust, there he is unjust."[6] To illustrate, he tells the story of Gyges, a shepherd in Lydia, who finds a ring that when worn and turned inward toward his hand makes him invisible, his presence unknown. Using this power, he is able to seduce the queen of Lydia, kill the king, and take the kingdom for himself with no one ever suspecting him.

What the drow wouldn't give for a ring like that! A sphere of magical silence to eliminate the sound of an approaching army is good. A spell to conjure up warm air to hide an assassin's body heat from the infrared sight of fellow drow is even better. But a ring that makes one invisible and undetectable about takes the cake, especially when plotting a raid on a powerful House. House Do'Urden's raid on House Devir would have been much simpler with the Ring of Gyges. Weapons master Zaknafein could have just walked right into the mushroom grove, levitated over the walls and into the prayer room, slaughtered all of the nobles capable of accusing him and his House of attempted murder, and walked out a hero, no casualties. The eight other higher-ranked houses would be dumbstruck by the event, and the drow's evil deity Lolth the Spider Queen would have to bestow good graces a-plenty on House Do'Urden (or maybe not…she is pretty vile and has some angst about Houses becoming too powerful).

Injustice served, right? Too bad it's just a myth. Wait, what am I saying?! It's a good thing no such ring exists because the consequences are terrifying! Doesn't a scene like this make justice more valuable than an annoying restraint against doing whatever we want? How could we ever live peacefully if a device like the Ring of Gyges was real? What's Glaucon's deal exactly?

"Creatures of survival, not of principle"

Glaucon is making a statement about people in general. He reasons that a person is only just because he or she fears the threat of retribution, but if that threat didn't exist then no one would behave justly. Suppose, as Glaucon does, that two Rings of Gyges existed, one worn by a perfectly just man and another worn by a perfectly unjust man.[7] Glaucon expects both men would succumb to the temptation to steal, kill, and commit any number of atrocities because they have no fear of retribution. We could argue fear of retribution is the only reason a city like Menzoberranzan still stands. Without it, its citizenry would be at each other's throats constantly until the whole race of dark elves eliminated itself. In fact, fear of retribution is the reason the drow maintain their power over all of the other creatures in the Underdark.

For example, on their way to see "justice" done against a house that failed to complete its raid, the Do'Urden party encounters some dwuergar, gray dwarves, who have blocked their path in the lane.[8] When the matron of House Do'Urden approaches, the dwarves initially turn on her angrily, but they hush up quick when they realize that a big mistake – crossing a high-ranking drow like Matron Malice – could result in an agonizing end. Thankfully, the dwarves have some resources, "crates of giant crab legs and other delicacies" they meant to trade in Menzoberranzan (you know you're poor when…), which they could use to appease the powerful drow matron before her daughter Briza uses her six-headed serpent whip against them. The dwarves pretty much knew they would be kissing half of their stock goodbye without a decent sale. Clearly, the drow wield the power of fear of retribution in the most wicked way to keep lesser creatures in line. It's a means of survival in a harsh world (more like a means to greedy ends, but what else could we expect from evil creatures?).

So is fear of retribution really the only way to think about justice? What about morality and being good-natured, living for something more than survival and "station"? Where's the love? It doesn't really exist in Menzoberranzan save for two individuals, and oh what lives they lead…

"I forgive your foolish thoughts … this time!"

The only two drow who seem to have a moral center are forced to hide it in the hell of their homeland. Zaknafein, weapons master of House Do'Urden and father to Drizzt, is haunted by living his double life of moral mass murderer. He takes great pains to conceal the reasoning for his true lust of killing drow – because they're evil. And of course Drizzt, the famous protagonist in the Dark Elf trilogy and much of the *Forgotten Realms* series, possesses an innate moral nature. Like father like son, it seems. Zak keeps a careful eye on his son and weapons protégé, worrying like crazy whether Drizzt will turn out evil like the rest of his kin (parents, right?). He almost decides to kill Drizzt during a sparring match the night before Drizzt is to go to the Academy to train as a fighter.[9] The thought of Drizzt, someone he has grown to care for deeply because of his similar moral nature, turning out just like the rest of the evil-spirited drow he has trained causes Zak severe pain. Drizzt feels similarly at the thought of his teacher's long list of kills and dishonorable methods of killing during raids. Drizzt feels the disappointment so strongly that he too considers murdering Zak in order to "remove himself from the wrongness around him."[10] (You know the old moral code: if you can't stand them being bad, take 'em out...hmm, something wrong there. Makes for good drama though!)

The fact that Zak and Drizzt live with such mental torment about the cruelty of drow society seems to prove Glaucon's point about justice being annoying. Since Zak and Drizzt have moral natures, that annoyance turns into a churning despair. Glaucon argues that truly just people are doomed to live wretchedly anyway simply because most people live otherwise, being just for the sake of appearances and not because they truly want to.

Let's say Zak and Drizzt stay in Menzoberranzan all their lives. Even if they could stay true to their principles, the tell-tale sign of a truly just person in Glaucon's perspective is a horribly wretched life. The test of the truly just man is to "let him be thought the worst (most unjust)"[11] and still retain his moral composure. In Menzoberranzan, the "worst" is flip-flopped such that being good and wholesome is "worst." If Zak and Drizzt showed their true nature, the fury of their family would descend upon them to beat it back down, even to the point of death. Zak and Drizzt manage to skirt around the "worst" by keeping it hidden, but they do bear the burden of watching their ruthless race behave so maliciously without calling foul. Drizzt's resolve is strongly tested when he learns that on the night of his birth "House DeVir ceased to exist" at the hands of his own family, and his own brother Dinin became the firstboy of the house by murdering Nalfein.[12] In a way, Drizzt's life is the result of the unjust nature of his race. He would have been sacrificed to Lolth as is customary for third-born sons were it not for Dinin's perfect execution. Unfortunately Zak and Drizzt have to learn to hold their tongues and accept the stinging reality of their surroundings – when it comes to clean kills and annihilation without a trace, "it never happened."[13]

The just person is an idiot for choosing justice, especially in the world of the drow. Compassion has no place in Menzoberranzan, and whenever Matron Malice, Briza, Dinin, or any of the members of House Do'Urden catch a hint of it from Zak or Drizzt, they become suspicious and agitated. During his first grand melee at the Academy, Drizzt completely embarrassed his brother Dinin, a master at the school, when Drizzt proved himself "a good fool"[14] by trusting another competitor, only to be turned on toward the end of the battle. And when Drizzt suggested using reason to handle a potential raid on the house, Matron Malice violently responded to his insolence.[15]

Moral people may also threaten a House's good standing with the evil Lolth, so they are especially dangerous. On a surface raid, Drizzt, horrified and outraged by the massacre of unarmed surface elves, not only hides a young elf from the slaughter but also maims a drow warrior in an instinctive reaction of disgust.[16] Drizzt covers his actions well, but the Spider Queen apparently sees everything and loses all favor for House Do'Urden, alerting Matron Malice. Suspicions about Drizzt and Zak lead Malice to spy on the two to learn once and for all their true natures. Shocked and angry, Malice resolves to kill Drizzt and later Zak, who elects to take his place.

Despite the violence and the twisted visions of reality (because those things can so easily be tossed aside …), perhaps the warped vision of "justice" does work to some degree in Menzoberranzan. The people manage not to kill each other to the point of a ruined society. When they do kill they make sure no one finds out, or "justice" really is served. All manner of beings are kept in their place through fear, and morality is silenced from the start or eliminated if it ever appears. If it ain't broke, I suppose … Still, Menzoberranzan is such an unsatisfactory vision of a just state that something must be missing.

"What do you see that the rest of us cannot?"

The trouble with flat-out calling Menzoberranzan the most unjust state imaginable is that it has some qualities befitting a just state. In the *Republic*, the philosopher Socrates is depicted as the good-guy character. He responds to Glaucon's and others' disbelief in the goodness of justice by directing their attention to the bigger picture, the state. He thus envisions what a perfectly just state would look like. Notably, Socrates says that "one man should practice one thing only, the thing to which his nature was best adapted."[17] Drow society is all about keeping things in their proper place. Initially, Matron Malice desires to prepare Drizzt to become the House's new wizard to replace Nalfein. But Zak intervenes and demonstrates Drizzt's unbelievable skill at coin-flipping, a sign he should train to be a fighter.[18] The same rule applies across the genders in Menzoberranzan – females are trained to become high priestesses to the Spider Queen while the males typically focus on fighting and magic for battle purposes.

Socrates also says that justice in the ideal state involves doing one's own business and not being a busybody – in other words, there would be no meddling in affairs that were not one's own in a just state.[19] Meddling in stuff one has no business meddling in is a quick way to earn a sharp glance or worse in Menzoberranzan. Consider an example involving the fake Faceless One, Alton DeVir. In order to learn of the guilty House that destroyed his, Alton dips into some evil divination, a practice reserved for high priestesses. He contacts another plane to speak to his dead mother, Matron Ginafae, but he does not realize that her soul is in the hellish torment of the Abyss.[20] Before he acquired the name of the guilty House, a hideous yochlol, handmaiden to the Spider Queen Lolth, appeared and spewed forth a wave of hungry spiders at the deformed mage, forcing him to drop a fireball at his own feet (what, no magic spell to concoct a cloud of Raid?). Alton's fiery lesson-learned is an extreme case, but it drives home the point of sticking to what you're good at and not meddling. The drow are very concerned with staying focused and ensuring others are as well. Drizzt is regularly admonished to learn his place, usually as he his engaging in some backtalk or raising questions. Questions are a form of meddling and therefore taken quite seriously, not just as a social breach but as an endangerment to the structure of society.

In addition to justice, Socrates calls for the ideal state and its citizens to embody the virtues of temperance, wisdom, and courage. Maybe the drow do have a well-disciplined society, but it in no way effectively creates or preserves temperance, wisdom, and courage (reasonable resolve).[21]

"His companions ... viewed their surroundings through tainted eyes"

Temperance is definitely out. Even though the drow manage to stay their weapons long enough for the right moment to strike, they are still driven by their lust for power. The drow live forever unsatisfied – even the first-ranked House Baenre has to concern itself with remaining well fortified against the lesser houses. And the whole task of fine-tuning their greediness is enhanced with balancing favor with the Spider Queen. The city itself is an incubator of intemperate souls engaged in a vicious game of king of the mountain.

Wisdom is lacking in Menzoberranzan. Since questioning is taboo, there is no impetus for self-realization. None of Drizzt's siblings give a thought to their place in Menzoberranzan, let alone within the greater universe of the *Forgotten Realms*. The Academy does nothing to encourage otherwise. Drizzt gives a scathing account of what exactly the Academy is: "the propagation of the lies that bind drow society together, the ultimate perpetuation of falsehoods."[22] The master of lore Hatch'net delivers sermons about the evils of the faeries and the surface world, the merciful grace of the Spider Queen, and other "hate rhetoric" designed to convince the drow of their superior nature and encourage their belief that the world must be conquered. Hatch'net is even prized for it by House matrons! In sum, wisdom is not cultivated in Menzoberranzan because the goal is station, not understanding.

Lastly, courage is hardly a sustainable virtue in drow society for a number of reasons. Traditionally speaking, the drow have nothing heroic to say of themselves. They live to survive and thrive off the kill. They demonstrate a certain chutzpah when they attempt to bring down a whole House, but the raids are well calculated to the point where bringing it down is almost an inevitability, and in the event of failure it is more of a gamble, not a matter of courage. Plus, the drow are pretty much the masters of the Underdark; when they go patrolling, we wouldn't really ever say they were in any kind of danger (unless we were talking about a complete klutz on the battlefield).

But to really have a mind for why courage dies in Menzoberranzan, we have to realize how courage works in tandem with wisdom. In reference to courage in the state, Socrates compares courage to a kind of "salvation," meaning a preservation of the opinion of things to be feared.[23] When the patrolling drow raid the surface, they are commended for striking out some of the evils they believe to exist against them. They are also well lauded for staying out until dawn to have their retinas seared by a sun they have never seen (like coming out of a movie theatre, only ten thousand times worse!). Still, to call their acts courageous loses some luster when we know those acts are guided by a well-ingrained ignorance of both themselves and their world. Menzoberranzan raises some extremely powerful creatures, but none of them preserve the virtues of temperance, wisdom, or courage. Well, save for the weirdo with the purple eyes.

"How I wish that one had learned his place, his values"

It is a wonder someone like Drizzt could ever come out of such an unjust home as Menzoberranzan. Despite living in a city packed with beings fueled by selfish desires who kowtow to an evil Spider Queen, Drizzt maintains his core values right up to the point of challenging his own family. Just before making his escape into exile, Drizzt demonstrates the core values sustained by a just state. He shows great character by temperately sparing his family the wrath of his scimitars (let's just agree the unsuspecting members would not have had time to react to

Drizzt's lightning attacks; he managed to knock off two wizards before facing his family after all …). His wisdom is seen through his ceaseless resolve to question. As he makes his way to face his family, Drizzt is intent on uncovering the true nature of Zaknafein by suggesting they both escape from Menzoberranzan, not knowing Matron Malice had killed him. Thus, in order to learn of Zak's "tormented soul" and ultimate sacrifice to save him, Drizzt interrogates Malice about Zak's final moments. He gains a full understanding of the evils of his family, his race, and the utter injustice of his home. Finally, he shows courage by facing the biggest threats to his existence, yet he does not blindly attack them – quite the opposite really, tossing down one of Zak's orbs of light to sear the eyes of his brethren in order to make an escape![24] Drizzt preserves the opinion that his family is truly evil, an opinion guided by reason and consideration of the actions and characters of Matron Malice, Briza, Dinin, and the rest.

By cultivating the virtues of his character, Drizzt does an injustice to his homeland (which is to do justice!). He proves that out of something so grievously unjust, a just being can spring. But he cannot stay there. To live in such a hellish place as Menzoberranzan while at the core possessing a strong sense of justice would be a nightmare and eventually lead to death. Drizzt is the exception, not the rule. So as the only moral dark elf leaves the pitch-black city of his birth, it is safe to assume Menzoberranzan continues on as a perfect unjust state.

Notes

1. R.A. Salvatore, *Homeland* (Renton, WA: Wizards of the Coast, 2004).
2. Ibid., p. 148.
3. Ibid., p. 113.
4. Plato, *Republic*, trans. Benjamin Jowett (New York: Barnes & Noble, 2004). It is crucial to note Plato's writing style here. He writes in dialogue form, like a play, usually with Socrates as the primary speaker or lesson-giver.
5. Ibid., pp. 39–41.

6. Ibid., p. 42.

7. Ibid.

8. Salvatore, *Homeland*, pp. 109–110.

9. Ibid., pp. 126–129.

10. Ibid., p. 236.

11. Plato, *Republic*, p. 43.

12. Salvatore, *Homeland*, p. 166.

13. Ibid., p. 168; the ability to fabricate reality and simultaneously live according to truth is pretty twisted, but it raises a strong question about the nature of reality. For instance, who is the real Dinin? The one who murdered his older brother and became firstboy? Or the one who ascended to the position because of Nalfein's untimely demise during a raid? The choices are twisted because, essentially, they are the same! Yet one condemns Dinin while the other doesn't. So as far as drow society (chooses to) believe, the latter choice is the real Dinin, but he isn't *really*.

14. Ibid., p. 146.

15. Ibid., p. 197.

16. Ibid., pp. 227–228.

17. Plato, *Republic*, p. 132.

18. Salvatore, *Homeland*, pp. 71–73.

19. Plato, *Republic*, p. 132; we need to frame what Socrates says here within the context of the rest of the *Republic*. In creating the perfect state, Socrates ultimately fashions one ruled by philosopher-kings, people who consigned themselves to the love of wisdom and the search for truth. The philosopher kingdom ousted all others, including recognizable governments of today, and one of the reasons is because in those other governments average people have the authority to meddle in state affairs and in the lives of citizens. This criterion sort of grows out of the first one: Socrates affirms to the common people: *stick to what you're good at.*

20. Salvatore, *Homeland*, pp. 82–84.

21. A really good breakdown of how the virtues figure into Socrates' perfect state is up on the web via Dr. Tobias Hoffmann, Associate Professor of Philosophy at the Catholic University of America. Available at http://faculty.cua.edu/hoffmann/courses/201_1068/Plato-5%20Republic.4.pdf. Accessed March 23, 2014.

22. Salvatore, *Homeland*, p. 133.

23. Plato, *Republic*, p. 128.

24. Salvatore, *Homeland*, pp. 319–320.

10

Who Is Raistlin Majere?

Kevin McCain

Dungeons & Dragons is full of great heroes and villains. The many worlds of the *D&D* multiverse are overflowing with them – from heroes such as the twin-scimitar-wielding drow Drizzt Do'Urden and the self-sacrificing knight Sturm Brightblade to villains such as the lord of Barovia, the vampire Count Strahd Von Zorovich, Vecna, the lich who rose to demi-godhood, and countless others. However, there is one that stands above all others. Who is this? Well, several names might come to mind when you consider this question. But only one is correct. No, it's not Elminster! It is the Master of Past and Present, Raistlin Majere.[1] Villain? Maybe. Tragic hero? Perhaps. Most powerful wizard in *D&D*? Absolutely! According to the death knight Lord Soth, "Of all of the living I have ever met, he is the only one I fear."[2] What other wizard can claim to strike fear into Lord Soth? Or have the Dark Queen, Takhisis, refer to him as "my worthy opponent" and bow to him in respect – "And I bow to you, Raistlin"?[3] Exactly, none.[4]

For a small taste of what makes Raistlin so incredible consider the following. He completed the potentially deadly Test of High Sorcery, which all wizards on Krynn seeking to advance beyond a novice level of power must pass, at an extremely young age. He was responsible for allowing Tanis Half-Elven to kill Ariakas, the leader of the dragonarmies, and for stopping the

Dungeons & Dragons and Philosophy: Read and Gain Advantage on All Wisdom Checks, First Edition. Edited by Christopher Robichaud.
© 2014 John Wiley & Sons, Inc. Published 2014 by John Wiley & Sons, Inc.

Dark Queen from entering the world – effectively ending the War of the Lance. He traveled through time to learn from and ultimately outwit the most powerful archmage in the history of Krynn, Fistandantilus. He journeyed to the Abyss and defeated the Dark Queen, becoming a god himself. After defeating Takhisis he proceeded to do what she always wanted to, but never could, destroy all the other gods. Ultimately, he was left to rule over Krynn alone – that's right the hourglass constellation stood alone in the sky (of course, in the end he decided not to defeat Takhisis because he learned of the ultimate outcome of his becoming a god).[5] He was integral in the defeat of Chaos – without his help his nephew Palin Majere wouldn't have had access to the necessary spell. Finally, he did what none of the gods of Krynn could do – he found the world when the Dark Queen transported it to another galaxy and hid it from them. This is just a sampling of the incredible things that Raistlin did. How can you describe him? In a word, "awesome"!

Although one could write books describing the amazing feats that Raistlin accomplished (in fact people have), chronicling his tales is not our concern here. Our concern here is with a seemingly simple question: who is Raistlin Majere? Of course, he is the brother of Caramon Majere. He is the wizard with golden skin and hourglass pupils. He is the Master of Past and Present. But, who is he? That is, what makes it true that it was a single person that accomplished all of the extraordinary feats that Raistlin did?

The Question and the Test

Our question is a philosophical one. It is a question that sits at the heart of metaphysics (the philosophical study of the nature of reality). It is the question of what makes a person the same person over time. What makes you the same person now as you were a year ago? Ten years ago? A month from now? Ten years from now? By exploring the question of who Raistlin Majere is, perhaps we can shed some light on the question of who we are.

This question is what philosophers call the "persistence question" of personal identity. It is the question of what conditions are required for a person at one time to be *numerically identical* to a person at a different time. To say of A and B that they are numerically identical is to say that A is B (they are one and the same thing – there really aren't two things at all, but rather just one). This is very different from *qualitative identity*. Qualitative identity is the sort of identity that identical twins could have – not twins like Caramon and Raistlin, but identical twins that cannot be told apart. Although twins of this sort cannot be told apart, they are separate entities. Thus, it is possible for things to be qualitatively identical, but not numerically identical. It is also possible for things to be numerically identical without being qualitatively identical. For example, when Raistlin fights in the War of the Lance he has white hair, golden skin, and hourglass pupils, but when he travels back in time he has brown hair, pale skin, and regular pupils – Raistlin at these different times is numerically identical, but not qualitatively identical. Similarly, you are numerically identical to the person who you were five years ago, but you are not qualitatively identical. After all, if we could place you and your past self in the same room, it would be possible to tell you apart.

Our question concerns the conditions of numerical identity. So, when we ask "Who is Raistlin Majere?" we are asking what makes it the case that the golden-skinned, white-haired, hourglass-eyed Raistlin who fought Takhisis in the Abyss is numerically identical to the pale-skinned, brown-haired, brown-eyed Raistlin who was hanging around Istar at the time of the Kingpriest.

Now one might be tempted to say that there is an easy answer to this question: these Raistlins aren't the same. It wasn't one person who performed all of the feats that are attributed to Raistlin. This would give us an easy answer to our question, but it wouldn't shed much light on what it is that makes *you* numerically identical to yourself when you were a child. Worse still, this answer would make it so that we shouldn't consider Raistlin to be such a great character. According to this answer to the question, there is no single person who accomplished everything that is credited to Raistlin. But, this easy answer is false. There is only one Raistlin and he did accomplish all of these feats. Any acceptable answer to our question must respect this truth. In fact, we will use the criterion of allowing for the same person, Raistlin, to accomplish his many feats as our test of theories. Fortunately, no one faces death for the failure of a theory to pass our test, as the mages do in the Towers of High Sorcery. But failure to pass our test does count as a serious problem for the theory.

Three Robes, Three Answers

It is fitting that the number of serious answers to the persistence question of personal identity is the same as the number of orders of magic, three. Just as, after the Test of High Sorcery, one must choose whether to take the white, red, or black robes, our test will allow us to choose whether to accept the somatic approach, the psychological approach, or anticriterialism.[6] Unlike the Conclave, we do not seek balance between our answers. We seek an answer that can account for Raistlin's identity, whether this can be accomplished by all three approaches or only one approach. Just as one should know about the orders before choosing one's robes, we should know the features of our three approaches to personal identity before submitting each to our test.

The *somatic approach* to the persistence question is the idea that personal identity is a physical relation. According to this approach, what makes you numerically identical with yourself as a child and yourself five years from now is that there is a kind of physical continuity that links you. One version of this approach says that you just are your body. So, what makes you the same person now as you were in the past has to do with the continuity that there is between your body now and your body in the past – your body now bears certain causal relations to your body in the past.[7] Another version of this approach says that you are the thinking animal that exists where you are.

According to this version of the somatic approach, what makes you the same person now as you were in the past is that you are the same animal – you are the same living organism now as you were then.[8]

The *psychological approach* holds that some psychological feature (or group of features) is what is necessary and sufficient for you to persist over time. One version of this approach is that you are identical with yourself of five years ago because you can remember experiences that you had five years ago.[9] It is fairly obvious that this view is problematic. It is plausible that if you are, say, 30 now, then you can remember experiences you had when you were 15. It is also plausible that when you were 15 you could remember experiences you had when you were 5. However, it is also plausible that you cannot now, at 30, remember the experiences you had when you were 5. If this is the case, then, according to this memorial version of the psychological approach, 5-year-old you is numerically identical to 15-year-old you and 15-year-old you is numerically identical to 30-year-old you, but 5-year-old you is not numerically identical to 30-year-old you. This is saying A = B and B = C, but A ≠ C. But, that is crazy! So, we won't consider the memory version of this approach when trying to determine who Raistlin Majere is. Instead, we will consider the more plausible version of this approach, where the condition that must be met for persistence is psychological continuity.[10] This version of the psychological approach says that the reason why you are the same person now as you were five years ago is that some of your mental states now are causally connected to mental states you had then. The idea is that you are the same person now as you were five years ago because at least some of your current mental states are what they are because of the mental states that you had five years ago.

Anticriterialism, as you might have guessed, is the view that there are no necessary and sufficient conditions for persistence. According to this approach, while certain features might provide evidence that one thing is numerically identical to another, there are no criteria that that must always be satisfied in order for a person to persist through time. So, while we might have evidence that suggests that you are the same person now as you were five years ago, there aren't criteria that guarantee that you are. That's not to deny that you are numerically identical to your younger self, but, rather, simply to claim that there isn't anything informative that can be said about what makes it the case that you are the same person now as you were in the past – you just are.[11]

Now that we have briefly explored the orders let's enter the tower and take the test.

Taking the Test

Raistlin presents a special challenge for any account of personal identity – not because of all of the incredible things that he did, but because of the extreme transformations that he went through. It is these transformations that pose the challenges for our test of theories. Let's consider the various approaches and see if they are able to handle the transformations that Raistlin underwent while maintaining that it is one person who completed all of the tasks that he did.

Let's start with anticriterialism. The test doesn't pose a challenge for this approach to personal identity at all. Since this approach denies that there are any criteria that are necessary or sufficient for persistence, no information that we provide about Raistlin's life (or his afterlife) can provide a reason for thinking that the anticriterialist approach fails our test. So, the test of anticriterialism is surely no Soulforge. It has the feel of theft over honest toil – it makes it too easy to get the result that Raistlin persists throughout all of his adventures. While we mentioned above that this is our ultimate test for the theories considered, anticriterialism should be our last resort because it tells us nothing about what it is that makes Raistlin persist. One must sacrifice something for the magic, that's part of the test – this approach sacrifices nothing and so it gains little power in return. Anticriterialism simply does not tell us what makes you the same person now as you were in the past and as you will be in the future. Thus, we should acknowledge that anticriterialism can pass the test in a sense, but we should definitely see if one of the other theories can as well because they could potentially tell us more about personal identity.

The somatic approach faces problems immediately. One of the first things we learn about Raistlin in the *Chronicles* is how his body has been drastically changed as a result of his experience with the Test of High Sorcery. After the Test of High Sorcery Raistlin's health is shattered (though always sickly he was never as bad as this), his hair has turned completely white, his skin is now a metallic gold, his skin tends to give off a feverish heat, and he now has hourglass-shaped pupils which cause him to see things as they age and decay. One might question how in the world Raistlin could be thought to have the same body before and after this experience. Even if we grant that somehow Raistlin's experiences in the Tower of High Sorcery didn't amount to his now having a different body, the somatic approach is still in trouble. When Raistlin travels through time to Istar at the time of the Kingpriest and then to Palanthas right after the Cataclysm, his body is different. He no longer has white hair, gold skin, and hourglass pupils – instead he has pale skin, brown hair, and brown eyes! As he himself exclaims "This face...His face! Not mine!"[12] According to the somatic approach, personal identity consists of either having the same body or being the same animal/physical creature. However, it is clear that when Raistlin travels through time he doesn't have the same body. Thus, the same-body version of this approach would pronounce that the Raistlin after his Test of High Sorcery is not identical to the person who existed back in the time of the Kingpriest. The body version of the somatic approach fails our test!

Can the animalist version of the somatic approach fare any better? One might try to make the case that although Raistlin's body goes through drastic changes, so much so that it isn't correct to say that he has the same body at different times, he is still the same animal/physical creature at these different times. This is very implausible. If Raistlin's body is completely different, it is very difficult to see how he could be the same *physical* animal. To make matters worse there is reason to think that at least sometimes Raistlin exists without a body at all. For example, when Caramon is trying to close the portal to the Abyss at the end of *Test of the Twins* he is unable to get the Staff of Magius to work – he simply can't get the portal to close. However, Raistlin's shadowy form appears next to him and touches the staff closing the Abyss while his body remains in the Abyss.[13] Here it seems that Raistlin exists without being a physical thing at all! Also, toward the end of the War of Souls it seems that it is Raistlin's spirit that helps the gods find Krynn. Since Raistlin exists at least at sometimes without a physical form at all, the somatic approach simply cannot pass our test.

The psychological approach can avoid the problems facing the somatic approach. According to the psychological approach, psychological continuity is both necessary and sufficient for a person to persist through time. So, the facts that Raistlin's body is very different at various times, that he has different bodies at different times, and that he seems to exist at some times without a body at all pose no problem for this approach. All that is required for Raistlin to be the same person throughout all of the various adventures he has is that there is psychological continuity between him at any given time with how he was at earlier times. So long as the mental states that Raistlin has at a particular time are the way they are largely because of mental states he had at earlier times he remains the same person throughout. This approach seems to have a good shot of passing the test.

But there may be a dark elf waiting to hurl a fireball at it. One of the most interesting things that Raistlin does is battle Fistandantilus and not only destroy him, but take his life force, all of his knowledge, and all of his magic powers. This creates a bit of a puzzle for the psychological approach, however. After Raistlin defeats Fistandantilus, his mental states are very different – so different that he asks, "Who am I?"[14] In fact Raistlin has some difficulty distinguishing between his original memories and those of Fistandantilus. As he says, "I see people that I've never seen, yet I know them!"[15] He also explains, "I have never been here, yet I have walked these halls...I am a stranger, yet I know the location of every room."[16] Can Raistlin's mental states really have the continuity required in order for the Raistlin before his final confrontation with Fistandantilus to be numerically identical with the Raistlin that absorbs Fistandantilus' life-force, knowledge, and magical might? Though it might sound strange, it does seem that his mental states can have the requisite continuity. After all, what is required on the psychological approach is that Raistlin's mental states after his victory be the way they are largely because of his earlier mental states. It seems that his mental states do have this feature – he still knows things from his childhood, the things that he did growing up, his actions during the War of the Lance, and, further, he still has similar emotional reactions toward people he knows like his brother Caramon and the priestess, Crysania. Thus, although there are some challenges for the psychological approach, it seems like it can account for what makes Raistlin the same person throughout his adventures. Perhaps this approach doesn't quite make it through the test without some burns, but no one does.

Unfortunately, like the Test of High Sorcery, things are not always how they at first seem. There is a major problem for the psychological approach. Raistlin after his final encounter with Fistandantilus is psychologically continuous with Raistlin before their battle, so on the psychological approach they are numerically identical. So far, so good. However, Raistlin after the battle with Fistandantilus is also psychologically continuous with Fistandantilus before the fight. Raistlin's mental states after this encounter are the way they are largely because of the way Fistandantilus' mental states were before the encounter. After all, Raistlin absorbs all of Fistandantilus' knowledge and memories! So, the psychological approach would say that Fistandantilus before the battle and Raistlin after the battle are numerically identical. At first this may not seem to be a problem because many question who really won this battle – some even think that Fistandantilus won (they're wrong, of course, but there's no need to get into that here). Yet there is a significant problem. We know that Raistlin before the battle and Fistandantilus before the battle are not numerically identical. They are clearly two different people. The psychological approach is committed to claiming that Raistlin after the battle is numerically identical to both Fistandantilus before the battle and Raistlin before the battle. But, clearly Fistandantilus before the battle and Raistlin before the battle are not identical. So, we have one thing, Raistlin after the battle, which is identical to two other things that are not identical to one another. In other words the psychological approach is committed to claiming that $A = B$ and $A = C$, but $B \neq C$. This cannot be correct! So, unless there is some way for the psychological approach to plausibly maintain that Raistlin after the battle is not numerically identical to Fistandantilus before the battle, it cannot pass our test. It is not clear that there is such a way.

The Master of Past and Present

We have seen that the somatic approach clearly cannot pass our test. We have seen that the psychological approach doesn't seem to be able to pass the test either. So we are left with anticriterialism. However, anticriterialism doesn't really give us much of an answer to our question. Perhaps that is all we can hope for – certain things are evidence that Raistlin persists throughout his many achievements. Likewise, certain things are evidence that you are the same person now as you were five years ago, but there simply aren't necessary and sufficient conditions for numerical identity. Where does this leave us with respect to our question? Who is Raistlin Majere? Perhaps all we can say is that he is the Master of Past and Present. He is the greatest *D&D* character ever (deal with it!). Perhaps that is all we can say. Perhaps it is enough.

Appendix
Tales of Raistlin

This is a list of the novels in which Raistlin plays a role. There are also short stories about him, but these are the core of the canon written by creator Margaret Weis.

Key

* Raistlin is the main character of the work

\# Raistlin is discussed significantly in the work, but also significantly shares the spotlight

! Raistlin plays an important role (of course!), but is not mentioned a lot in the work

Before the War of the Lance

The Raistlin Chronicles

*The Soulforge by Margaret Weis

**The Brothers Majere* by Margaret Weis and Don Perrin

War of the Lance

Chronicles

\#*Dragons of Autumn Twilight* by Margaret Weis and Tracy Hickman

\#*Dragons of Winter Night* by Margaret Weis and Tracy Hickman

\#*Dragons of Spring Dawning* by Margaret Weis and Tracy Hickman

The Lost Chronicles

\#*Dragons of the Dwarven Depths* by Margaret Weis and Tracy Hickman

\#*Dragons of the Highlord Skies* by Margaret Weis and Tracy Hickman

Dragons of the Hourglass Mage by Margaret Weis and Tracy Hickman

Post-War of the Lance

Legends (this is the heart of the story of Raistlin)

Time of the Twins by Margaret Weis and Tracy Hickman
War of the Twins by Margaret Weis and Tracy Hickman
Test of the Twins by Margaret Weis and Tracy Hickman

War with Chaos

! *Dragons of Summer Flame* by Margaret Weis and Tracy Hickman

War of Souls

(Raistlin doesn't really play much of a role in the first two books, but he is in the third)

Dragons of a Fallen Sun by Margaret Weis and Tracy Hickman
Dragons of a Lost Star by Margaret Weis and Tracy Hickman
! *Dragons of a Vanished Moon* by Margaret Weis and Tracy Hickman

Notes

1. Margaret Weis and Tracy Hickman, *Time of the Twins* (Renton, WA: Wizards of the Coast, 2011); Margaret Weis and Tracy Hickman, *War of the Twins* (Renton, WA: Wizards of the Coast, 2011); and Margaret Weis and Tracy Hickman, *Test of the Twins* (Renton, WA: Wizards of the Coast, 2011). All references to these books are to the e-book format.

2. *Test of the Twins*, p. 72.
3. Ibid., p. 145.
4. If you don't know about Raistlin, then I recommend that you immediately (that's right *immediately*!) get started on reading the items listed above in the appendix to this chapter.
5. In order to really appreciate the importance of this it is necessary to realize that *DragonLance* is not like the *Forgotten Realms*. In the *Forgotten Realms* campaign setting, while it is not common that a mortal arises to godhood, it is not unheard of and it has happened many times. In the *DragonLance* campaign setting this simply doesn't happen – no mortal becomes a god. Well, no mortal, other than Raistlin Majere.
6. These terms for the categories of responses are from Eric T. Olson, "Personal Identity," in Edward N. Zalta, ed., *The Stanford Encyclopedia of Philosophy*, (Winter 2010 edn.). Available at http://plato.stanford.edu/archives/win2010/entries/identity-personal/. Accessed March 23, 2014. The interested reader is encouraged to consult Olson's article for a more detailed discussion of the general issues of personal identity.
7. For more on this view see A.J. Ayer, *Language, Truth, and Logic* (London: Gollancz, 1936).
8. For development and defense of this view see Eric T. Olson, *The Human Animal: Personal Identity without Psychology* (Oxford: Oxford University Press, 1997).
9. As Olson (ibid.) notes, this view is sometimes attributed to John Locke, but it is doubtful that Locke actually held this view of personal identity.
10. This view has been developed to a large extent by Sydney Shoemaker, "Personal Identity: A Materialist's Account," in Sydney Shoemaker and Richard Swinburne, *Personal Identity* (Oxford: Blackwell, 1984), pp. 67–132.
11. This view has been defended by Trenton Merricks, "There Are No Criteria of Identity Over Time," *Noûs* 32 (1998), pp. 106–124.
12. *War of the Twins*, p. 149.
13. *Test of the Twins*, p. 265.
14. *War of the Twins*, p. 43.
15. Ibid., p. 149.
16. Ibid., p. 320.

Part V

THE ETHICS OF SPELLCASTING

11

Expediency and Expendability
An Exhumation of the Morality of Necromancy

Matthew Jones and Ashley Brown

Necromancy within the context of *Dungeons & Dragons* is a powerful and versatile school of spells relying on negative energy. This chapter will focus on the archetypal image of the necromancer: the black-robed creator and master of the undead. The necromancer is often depicted as a mere cackling villain, using her power over death to forward her evil agenda. In this way, necromancy has been philosophically maligned. Although necromancers were traditionally considered to be evil in *D&D*, the game came to accommodate the idea that necromancers, in theory, could be neutral, or even good-aligned, with their powers used for the greater good.

Perhaps due to the nature of their trade, necromancers have been unfairly given a bad reputation. Although for most creatures evil is a choice, for necromancers and their minions evil is a label unfairly slapped upon them. The quintessential necromantic spell, *animate dead*, has the [evil][1] descriptor for seemingly no other reason than its dealings with undeath. These descriptors of evil spells and evil creatures are theoretically unjustifiable.

Dungeons & Dragons and Philosophy: Read and Gain Advantage on All Wisdom Checks, First Edition. Edited by Christopher Robichaud.

To combat this, however, we cannot appeal to moral anti-realism, the belief that objective moral truths do not exist, because *Dungeons & Dragons* is a moral realist work. To speak of good and evil within the context of the game is to speak of objective truths, the existence of which can be demonstrated beyond doubt or question. By means of various spells and abilities, for example a paladin's *detect evil*,[2] the moral character of an individual or action can be assessed.

When considering this absolutism of morality in *Dungeons & Dragons*, it is not reasonable to place necromancy, and the animation of mindless undead, on a list of things that are inherently evil. The distaste for necromancy and its mindless minions is instead a relic of "pre-theoretical intuition" – a common-sense belief that may not hold up to philosophical scrutiny. Our cultural conceptions of the undead revolve around flesh-eating viruses, evil books of necromantic power, tentacled abominations from beyond the stars, and the voracious eating of brains. So it's easy to miss the fact that the mindless undead which *Dungeons & Dragons* presents us with are qualitatively different and rather more benign.

From Killing to Kant:
Exploring the [Evil] Descriptor

The *Player's Handbook* states evil "implies hurting, oppressing, and killing others" and that "evil characters and creatures debase or destroy innocent life, whether for fun or profit."[3] Taken at face value, these statements are non-contentious. However, a computer role-playing game adapted from *Dungeons & Dragons*, *Baldur's Gate II: Shadows of Amn*, features a quest in which a paladin and their party can be tricked into murdering a band of lawful good knights, each group being perceived by the other as marauding ogres. In this instance, a good character is performing what would normally be considered an evil action – yet this presumably would not cause them to fall to evil.

This suggests that the moral properties of an action derive at least in part from the intention of the person acting. This interpretation is further supported by the class description of the paladin, which states that a paladin who "willfully commits an evil act, or who grossly violates the code of conduct loses all paladin spells and abilities."[4] The word *willfully* is significant, as it allows for an act performed with good intentions to lead to evil consequences without itself being an evil act. The plight of the paladin is illustrative of an important conflict in ethical theory: the conflict between deontological, duty-based and utilitarian, outcome-based ethical theories.

The paladin's code of ethics is deontological in that they must abide by a strict code of conduct. To an extremely strict deontologist, an action's moral status is entirely independent of its consequences. A famous example that demonstrates this is Immanuel Kant's (1724–1804) "inquiring murderer."[5] Kant argues that it is always wrong to tell a lie, even when faced with a wild-eyed and axe-wielding murderer looking for a friend who is hiding in our house. Kant justifies this in part by arguing that the consequences of actions can never be known, so a lie may result in the murderer succeeding in his task while telling the truth might have allowed our friend time to escape. Also, a lie is by definition parasitic upon the concept of truth-telling – a lie can only be believed so long as people are generally considered to be truthful. If lying were the norm, then no statement would be trusted as factually correct. Lying, therefore, is always wrong as it makes a contribution – even a small one – towards a state where no one is trusted at all.

Utilitarian theories of ethics contrast with Kant's deontological approach. To see how, let's consider a particularly contentious contemporary ethical dilemma, the ticking bomb scenario, which posits that an explosive has been hidden in a major population center. A suspect has been captured who knows where the bomb is and how to disarm it, yet he remains uncooperative. Is it permissible to then use torture? For the purposes of this chapter, the bomb could be replaced with a magical explosive or gnomish steam-powered doomsday machine, and the scenario's dilemma would remain unchanged. In Kantian terms, a paladin may well be prohibited from torturing a helpless captive or telling a lie, regardless of the circumstances.

According to act utilitarianism, actions that result in maximized happiness for all those involved can be justified, no matter how gruesome. In act utilitarianism, it would be acceptable to torture the suspect if there was a certainty, or even a sufficient probability (depending on just how torture-happy an act utilitarian we're imagining) of being able to learn how to disarm the device. Equally, a reasonable utilitarian person might well believe that lying to the blood-drenched and axe-wielding inquiring murderer will result in a far better outcome (and a far smaller cleaning bill!) than telling the truth.

The [evil] descriptor is deontological rather than utilitarian. Inherently evil actions often involve such things as the deliberate, and unnecessary, infliction of pain. A distinction can be drawn here between the spells *imprisonment*[6] and *eternity of torture*.[7] While both permanently disable a character, one does so by putting them in stasis, while the other inflicts agony upon them. Other [evil] spells in *Dungeons & Dragons* include those related to the service of evil deities, the summoning of demons, and those otherwise concerned with advancing the cause of evil. These things are held to be bad in all cases. If *animate dead* is to be placed in the same theoretical class as spells such as *eternity of torture,* then it must, in some way, cause harm, or otherwise serve the cause of evil.

The Ghost in the Machine: The Dualism of *Dungeons & Dragons*[8]

Typical *D&D* cosmology is explicitly dualist in that there is a soul/body divide. Bodies exist, and souls also exist. As stated in the *Player's Handbook*, "when a living creature dies, its soul departs its body, leaves the Material Plane, travels through the Astral Plane, and goes to abide on the plane where the creature's deity resides."[9] Equally, by means of spells such as *magic jar,* the soul can be temporarily removed from the body. In terms of a theory of personal identity, this is nonreductionist – which means that which gives a person their quality of personhood cannot be explained solely in terms of facts about brains and bodies, instead requiring facts about a soul. This contrasts with reductionism, which is the belief that mental phenomena can be reduced to physical phenomena.[10]

To begin, let us consider the rather morbid example of Tordek the fighter.[11] In an epic battle, Tordek was killed and dismembered. If we wanted to give life, or undeath, to Tordek's abused corpse, the rules of *Dungeons & Dragons* provide us with a few options. *Raise dead* requires the body to be whole, or the raised creature will still be missing any parts that were not present upon its return to life. *True resurrection*, on the other hand, doesn't require the body at all – it merely requires that the caster can positively identify the creature to be resurrected. This is significant, for it calls to mind contemporary developments in the philosophy of religion and identity.

In one such development, Peter van Inwagen, in "The Possibility of Resurrection," gave the example of a manuscript originally written by St. Augustine. This manuscript was "burned by Arians in the year 457," yet God miraculously re-created it in 458.[12] Van Inwagen argues that we intuitively reject the idea of the copy being the same manuscript as the original, given that it never knew the impress of St. Augustine's hand. It is at best an exact copy, akin to a house of blocks that has been knocked over and rebuilt exactly as before. To paraphrase, he gives the following conversation to illustrate his point:

> "Is that the house of blocks your daughter built?"
> "No, I built this one after I accidentally knocked hers down.
> I put the blocks in the same place, though. Don't tell her."[13]

The same is true of the bodies of slain *D&D* characters. If Tordek were utterly obliterated by a wizard and then resurrected, the new body would be a copy of his previous body. However, due to the presence of the inhabiting soul, we would accept that continuity of identity is maintained between the two. This inference is further justified by the druid spell *reincarnate*. In the second edition *Player's Handbook*, *reincarnate* allows for dead characters to return to life as such things as badgers, wolverines, and owls. Even after this transformation, it is stated that "the person reincarnated recalls the majority of his former life and form."[14] So we can say, "this is Tordek," even after he has been reincarnated as an owl, but we can't so easily say, "this is Tordek the fighter," upon looking at a corpse, even one that has been reanimated.

This has some interesting theoretical implications. Not only does the soul survive the death of the body, but it survives in such a manner that its identity persists. If a character had access to planar magics, they would be able to travel to the plane upon which the soul of the deceased resides and speak with the now disembodied soul. The corpse is akin to a discarded suit of clothes, still retaining the imprinted knowledge that allows the *speak with dead* spell[15] to function, but entirely lacking the soul. This leads to the conclusion that the soul's quality of experience is not affected by the reanimation of the corpse and, therefore, that no direct harm is done to the deceased. Of course, we could say that harm is being done to the reanimated's friends and family, as seeing their loved one's corpse rise from the grave is surely shocking. This, though, would be due to the way in which we, as a culture, perceive death.

An obvious retort to the above points is that gods of death (and especially undeath!) are typically evil. *D&D* deities such as Vecna, Chemosh, and Velsharoon are quite clearly villains, and undeath is frowned upon by many good gods. However, an action cannot be considered evil merely because good gods disapprove of it. Plato (c.429–c.437 BCE) wrote of just such a problem in his dialogue between Socrates (469–399 BCE) and Euthyphro. Euthyphro, a high priest, was asked by Socrates to explain what made a pious action pious. He replied that piety reflected what was loved by the gods. However, being loved by the gods of goodness cannot make an action good, for that then makes goodness both arbitrary, when dependent upon a deity's free will, and potentially inconsistent. In the cases of both Plato and *Dungeons and Dragons*, different gods have different concepts of how one should behave. What is loved by one god might be detested by another. For objective moral truths to exist, they must exist above and beyond the wills of the gods.

The [Evil]ness of the Undead: Euthyphro Revisited

The *Monster Manual* states that zombies are "corpses reanimated through dark and sinister magic."[16] Again, this may seem like a non-contentious statement, but just what is it that makes the magic "dark and sinister"? The fact that the magic can be used to raise zombies would be an obvious answer, but this statement presupposes that zombies are evil. Likewise, skeletons are described as "mindless automatons that obey the orders of their evil masters."[17] What makes the masters evil? "Because they have skeletons," appears to be the feeble answer.

Once again, we have reached a logical circle. If the magic is dark because it raises zombies and skeletons, then this in turn has smuggled in its own implicit premise: that zombies and skeletons are evil and anything involving them is by definition also evil. The *Player's Handbook* explicitly states that "animals and other creatures incapable of moral action are neutral rather than good or evil."[18] Moral action is something that requires *agency*, or the capacity to act with intent, which disqualifies mindless creatures from being evil in their own right.

The Philosopher David Hume (1711–76) discussed such a problem in a much-quoted passage of *A Treatise on Human Nature*, arguing that statements of facts do not logically entail statements of moral properties. One cannot go from the proposition "necromancy involves animating the dead" to the proposition "necromancy is wrong" without implicitly accepting as true the further statement that "animating the dead is wrong." This then makes the statement "necromancy is wrong" tautologous, or true by definition, while being guilty of a logical error: the statement relies upon itself to demonstrate its own truth. From the descriptions of evil given to us by *Dungeons & Dragons* and the borrowed ideas of Hume, it becomes apparent that there is no logical justification for the consideration of necromantic acts as evil.

Necromancy for Fun and Profit: Some Examples Evaluated

To further explore the notion that necromancy is inherently an [evil] act, let's consider some examples. Philosophy thrives on trading examples and counter-examples in the attempt to demonstrate the adequacy or inadequacy of particular theories.

(1)   The 1999 computer role-playing game, influenced by the moral alignment system in *Dungeons & Dragons*, *Planescape: Torment* presented the idea of the Dustmen, a Sigil faction offering dubious contracts to the living. The Dustmen explain to potential contractors that in return for the use of their body after death for work in their mortuary, they will receive monetary payment. As this arrangement is entered into with open eyes and with no deception on the part of the necromancer, can this be said to be an evil act? Would the person who accepted such an offer be guilty of aiding the cause of evil? What if they use the money to buy medicine for their sick child? We intuitively perceive there to be a moral difference between, for example, signing a contract selling your soul to a demon and signing one to permit a necromancer to reanimate your corpse. It seems logical that willingly allowing an evil act would itself be morally dubious, but a villager signing a necromantic contract would not merit the same disapproval as one who sold their soul to Asmodeus.

(2)   A necromancer may use *animate dead* to prevent hardship befalling the living in a time of extreme circumstances. Consider the example of an adventuring party deep in hostile territory. Let's assume that Tordek the fighter and Jozan

the cleric have both been slain, leaving only Lidda the rogue and Mialee, a physically frail elven wizard. In this instance, is the wizard's use of *animate dead*, so as to allow the corpses to propel themselves towards resurrection, an evil act? After all, they have few alternatives.

(3)   To broaden the above example, let's consider the same adventuring party holed up in a small town besieged by a warband of hostile orcs. Many of the defenders have been killed by aggressive action, leaving a few brave men and women fighting a seemingly hopeless battle against a numerically superior foe. Mialee therefore casts *animate dead* to attempt to muster foot soldiers. As in example 1, the agreement of the defenders could be sought before their death, so the act would not be done against their will. Is this still an evil act?

(4)   Finally, necromancy can be used to save the living from danger or excessive hardship. For example, a lot of manual work conducted in the medieval period upon which *Dungeons & Dragons* is loosely based was extremely hazardous. If cheaply automated, this could result in a reduction in unnecessary death and suffering.

In the above four examples, circumstances have been manipulated and the reader granted background and insight into the specific conditions of a moral quandary. What this exercise in necromantic morality has demonstrated is that there are conditions in which it is possible for an "evil" act to be used for good. The larger, recurring, question of this chapter, about the true evil of necromancy, is once again raised.

Hobbes, Machiavelli, and a Necromancer Walk into a Bar...

As has been shown in the last two examples, strict adherence to deontological ethics may result in what Michael Walzer called a "[failure] to do the right thing (in utilitarian terms)."[19] To refuse to animate the dead on moral grounds could result in the permanent loss of one of Mialee's party members or, worse, the destruction of an entire town. War and politics especially are two realms where deontology and utilitarianism will frequently come into conflict. The examples under discussion reflect a situation where both possible outcomes can be considered "wrong" – so it is not easy to simply dismiss the use of necromancy as evil, especially when the alternative outcome is objectively worse. Indeed, the use of the dead could prevent the death of the living, which is hardly an evil aim.

Niccolò Machiavelli (1469–1527) was concerned with just this point in *The Prince* when he discussed Cesare Borgia, an Italian nobleman he states was "considered cruel."[20] Careful use of this cruelty, however, allowed him to "reconcile the Romagna" (a historical region of Italy much divided by political squabbles) and "restore it to peace."[21] Machiavelli contrasts Cesare's methods with those of the republic of Florence, which was facing a series of riots and revolts between two factions in Pistoia, a town that lay within their sphere of political influence. Rather than take the decisive action he advocated and restore order to the city by force, the Florentine republic elected to "avoid a reputation for cruelty" and continue attempting to broker a deal. This peace process was a dramatic failure, resulting in the collapse of government and the town's descent into total violent disorder. This example clearly demonstrates that doing the "right thing" in absolutist terms – obeying a deontological code of ethics – can at times lead to a dreadful outcome.[22] Hiding behind a strictly deontological code of ethics may allow for one's conscience to seem clear, but it does so at the cost of denying the true complexity of moral life. When faced with such a dilemma, one may not want the harsh rigidity of a paladin!

Thomas Hobbes (1588–1679) theorized about "the state of nature," the condition of humankind outside of civil society or in a time of a complete breakdown in order. His pessimistic assumptions about human nature led him to the conclusion that humanity's natural condition was "a state of war of all against all" – a state of affairs unpleasant enough that a rational person would want to avoid it at any cost.[23] A look at any modern failed state is enough to make this seem a reasonable statement – and it is only strengthened if, instead of merely being populated by humans, we imagine also facing the threat of illithids, dark elves, or evil wizards waiting to either enslave us or do to us a variety of other things too horrible to contemplate.

Walk like an Egyptian: Necromancy as Taboo and a "Possible World" Argument

So far we've seen that necromancy can at times be "the lesser evil." But can necromancy be further redeemed?

The term "possible world" refers to a particular species of metaphysical argument. There are said to be a limitless number of possible worlds, each representing a different way the world could have developed. Specifically, if a proposition is necessarily true, it must hold across all possible worlds, including those in *Dungeons & Dragons*. This contrasts with other types of truth which can be true across one or more possible worlds but false in others.

For example, it is necessarily true across all possible worlds that the circumference of a circle can be calculated by application of the formula Π D. Any world where this is not true would be distinctly Lovecraftian and, thus, not imaginable by the sane or those not initiated into the Cthulhu cult.

It is extremely difficult, though potentially not impossible, to imagine any possible world in which, for example, wanton slaughter or the use of *eternity of torture* could be considered inherently good actions. Both would explicitly violate the definition of [good] given in the *Dungeon Master's Guide*, not to mention many of our most deeply held social convictions.

The animation of mindless undead is disputably evil and does not belong in the same deontic category as the example of *eternity of torture*. As discussed earlier, no one need be directly harmed by such an action and it need not be done from selfish intentions. It is coherent to imagine a good god who condones the use of animated skeletons and zombies, perhaps one concerned with ancestor worship or one who promotes ideas of service to the community that continues even beyond death. It is even coherent to imagine one who explicitly approves of great leaders becoming intelligent undead and taking such forms as the arch-lich.[24]

So, our distaste for the undead must be reflective of our social and cultural norms. Sociologists have discussed this in terms of "habitus." Pierre Bourdieu defined habitus as a set of dispositions, behaviors, and values acquired through a remembered cultural history and experiential knowledge of the social world.[25] It is through habitus that we can understand our distaste for the undead as stemming from various cultural beliefs.

At one time, a fear, dislike, or repulsion relating to corpses may have developed through an association of dead bodies with the spread of pests, illness, or some other catastrophe. In contemporary times, an anachronized western European cultural memory of historical events such as the Black Death may somehow translate into a shared association of skeletons and corpses with disease, for example. Although we may share a popular cultural opinion that corpses are creepy, bad, or evil, as evidenced by the popularity of skeleton cut outs at Halloween, the original source for these sentiments has been lost somewhere in the stretch of time.

For an example of a real-world culture with a focus upon death which lacks stigmatization and association with plagues, we can turn to the ancient Egyptians, renowned for the pyramids and mummies. Osiris, a god of agriculture and irrigation, was slain by his brother Set at Abydos, and divided into sixteen parts. After his resurrection, Osiris also took on the role of judge of the dead – and the Egyptians believed that the mummified bodies of the dead would be physically resurrected just as Osiris was, becoming something closer to divine than mortal.[26] Explaining this with attention to habitus, we might say that Osiris' resurrection mirrors Egypt's own yearly rebirth following the Nile's bursting of its banks and giving water to crops.

We should note here that the Egyptian focus upon death does not suggest their society was joyless or morbid – perhaps surprisingly, Egyptologists assure us that "the elaborate death-culture of the Egyptians expresses ... a love of life."[27] It is possible, therefore, to have a culture with a significant focus on death that does not become either gloomy or sepulchral. It is possible for members of such a society to use necromancy without the necessity of an evil alignment. It is therefore possible to imagine a world in which necromancy is not inherently evil, but instead has associations of respect and reverence.

Hug a Zombie: Recognizing and Moving Beyond Our Cultural Prejudice

We are prejudiced against necromancy. This is doubly the case in the West, due in large part to a cultural history which sanctifies the corpse and vilifies those seeking to use it. This cultural legacy comes in part from the Bible. Necromancers are explicitly referred to several times as things that are abominable to God. There are explicit prohibitions in, amongst others, the books of Deuteronomy, Samuel, and Leviticus.[28] These prohibitions made the jump from religious text to law. The Code of Hammurabi, one of the oldest surviving codices of law, gives the punishment for "sorcery," which included magic working with the dead, as an ordeal by water.[29]

In addition to the cultural normativity taken from the Bible, *Dungeons & Dragons* also relies on its players' familiarity with anachronistic imaginings of medieval history. The setting and theme of *Dungeons & Dragons* reflects an idealized concept of medieval fantasy, with classes such as the paladin explicitly harking back to the notion of the chivalrous and divinely inspired crusading knight. Perhaps the quintessential work of medieval fantasy is Mallory's 1470 *Le Morte d'Arthur*, which features two major necromancers: Merlin and Morgan le Fay. Merlin is explicitly identified as being half-demon and is associated throughout the text with several signs of infernal temptation, his knowledge being stated by a knight to come from "the devil's craft." Morgan is stated to be "a great clerk of nigromancy [necromancy]"[30] and she launches multiple murderous magical attacks upon Arthur throughout the course of the work. This work, amongst others, helped to paint the image of the necromancer as the black-robed, monstrous figure.

The role of contemporary entertainment cannot be overlooked either. Films and TV series depict the walking dead as ravenous, brain-eating monstrosities. Next to such depictions, the relatively harmless nature of *Dungeons & Dragons'* mindless undead is easy to overlook. Animated by a morally neutral force rather than a book such as the *Necronomicon* or a mysterious virus, the skeletons and zombies of *Dungeons & Dragons* are more akin to constructs or tools than to the creatures of Hollywood and literature. Our brains, therefore, remain quite safe. If we can look beyond the green-tinged skin and the milky eyes of the undead, we can find a worthy and invaluable resource.

Notes

1. "Evil" and "good" are placed in square brackets in this chapter, as they are in *D&D* rulebooks, to make reference to the alignment system.
2. Although *detect evil* is innately a paladin ability, it is also a cleric spell. The spell's description reads: "You can sense the presence of evil. The amount of information revealed depends on how long you study a particular area or subject." Taken from Monte Cook, Jonathan Tweet, and Skip Williams, *Dungeons & Dragons Player's Handbook*, 3.5 edn. (Renton, WA: Wizards of the Coast, 2003), p. 218.
3. The full quotation is: "'Evil' implies hurting, oppressing, and killing others. Some evil creatures simply have no compassion for others and kill without qualms if doing so is convenient. Others actively pursue evil, killing for sport or out of duty to some evil deity or master" (ibid., p. 104).
4. Ibid., p. 44.

5. For a full definition of the "inquiring murderer" scenario, see Immanuel Kant, "Concerning a Pretended Right to Lie from Motives of Humanity" (1873), trans. A.E. Kroeger, *The Journal of Speculative Philosophy* 7, pp. 14–19. This paper was written in response to the French philosopher Benjamin Constant (1767–1830), who stated that Kant's categorical rejection of lying left him vulnerable to the "inquiring murderer" example while alleging that no one has the duty to tell a truth that causes obvious harm to another. In the work cited, Kant accepts Constant's example as valid while still maintaining that truthfulness was the morally correct response.

6. Cook et al., *Dungeons & Dragons Player's Handbook*, p. 244.

7. Monte Cook, *Book of Vile Darkness* (Renton, WA: Wizards of the Coast, 2002), pp. 93–94.

8. The title is taken from Gilbert Ryle's *The Concept of Mind*, in which he refers to the Cartesian soul with what he terms "deliberate abusiveness" as the "ghost in the machine." Gilbert Ryle, *The Concept of Mind* (London: Penguin Books, 2000), p. 17.

9. Cook et al., *Dungeons & Dragons Player's Handbook*, p. 171.

10. Kim Sterelny, "Reductionism in the Philosophy of Mind," in Edward Craig, ed., *The Shorter Routledge Encyclopedia of Philosophy* (Oxford: Routledge, 2005), p. 891.

11. Cook et al., *Dungeons & Dragons Player's Handbook*, p. 37.

12. Peter van Inwagen, "The Possibility of Resurrection," *International Journal for Philosophy of Religion* 9 (1978), pp. 114–121.

13. Ibid.

14. David Cook, *Advanced Dungeons & Dragons Player's Handbook* (Lake Geneva, WI: Tactical Studies Rules, 1995), pp. 296–297.

15. The spell text reads, "You grant the semblance of life and intellect to a corpse, allowing it to answer several questions that you put to it. You may ask one question per two caster levels. Unasked questions are wasted if the duration expires. The corpse's knowledge is limited to what the creature knew during life, including the languages it spoke (if any). Answers are usually brief, cryptic, or repetitive. If the creature's alignment was different from yours, the corpse gets a Will save to resist the spell as if it were alive. If the corpse has been subject to speak with dead within the past week, the new spell fails. You can cast this spell on a corpse that has been deceased for any amount of time, but the body must be mostly intact to be able to respond. A damaged corpse may be able to give

partial answers or partially correct answers, but it must at least have a mouth in order to speak at all."

16. Monte Cook et al., *Monster Manual*, 3rd edn. (Renton, WA: Wizards of the Coast, 2000), p. 192.

17. Ibid., p. 165.

18. Cook et al., *Dungeons & Dragons Player's Handbook*, p. 104.

19. Michael Walzer, "Political Action: The Problem of Dirty Hands," *Philosophy and Public Affairs* 2 (1973), pp. 160–180.

20. Niccolò Machiavelli, *The Prince* (Ware, Herts.: Wordsworth Editions, 1997), p. 64.

21. Ibid.

22. Ibid., p. 59.

23. Thomas Hobbes, *Leviathan* (New York: Oxford University Press, 1996), p. 403.

24. James Wyatt and Rob Heinsoo, *Monsters of Faerûn* (Renton, WA: Wizards of the Coast, 2001), p. 90.

25. Pierre Bourdieu, *Distinction: A Social Critique of the Judgement of Taste* (London: Routledge, 1984).

26. Stephen Quirke, *Ancient Egyptian Religion* (London: British Museum Press, 1992), p. 175.

27. John Casey, *After Lives: A Guide to Heaven, Hell and Purgatory* (Oxford: Oxford University Press, 2009), p. 23.

28. Isaiah 8: 19 (English Standard Version): "And when they say to you, 'Inquire of the mediums and the necromancers who chirp and mutter,' should not a people inquire of their God? Should they inquire of the dead on behalf of the living?" Also, Deuteronomy 18: 9–12 (English Standard Version): "When you come into the land that the Lord your God is giving you, you shall not learn to follow the abominable practices of those nations. There shall not be found among you anyone who burns his son or his daughter as an offering, anyone who practices divination or tells fortunes or interprets omens, or a sorcerer or a charmer or a medium or a necromancer or one who inquires of the dead, for whoever does these things is an abomination to the Lord. And because of these abominations the Lord your God is driving them out before you."

29. Robert Francis Harper, *Code of Hammurabi King of Babylon about 2250 B.C.*, 2nd edn. (Chicago: University of Chicago Press, 1904).

30. Thomas Malory, *Morte Darthur: Sir Thomas Malory's Book of King Arthur and of his Noble Knights of the Round Table* (London: Macmillan, 1868), p. 27.

By Friendship or Force
Is it Ethical to Summon Animals to Fight by Your Side in *Dungeons & Dragons*?

Samantha Noll

As anyone knows who has ever agonized over the *D&D Player's Handbook*, trying to decide the race, class, and alignment of a newborn character, particular classes have specific abilities that make them unique. For example, bards have the ability to lull an enemy to sleep with their songs or fortify the resolve of allies, and barbarians can fly into a rage during battle, dealing out massive amounts of damage to foes. In addition, several classes, such as rangers, mages, and druids, have the ability to call upon nonhuman animals for aid. The skill of calling animals to fight by your side brings up unique ethical questions.

In contrast to skills such as lock-picking and trap-making, for example, the ability to summon or call animals involves the participation of an individual that, depending on the particular animal and context, normally cannot give consent like a fellow adventurer could. Animals (whether they be mythical or common) have needs, desires, and, some argue, minds of their own.[1] They are beings living in the world, just was we are. If this were not so, then we wouldn't enjoy random encounters with them during the game. So the main question that we will attempt

Dungeons & Dragons and Philosophy: Read and Gain Advantage on All Wisdom Checks, First Edition. Edited by Christopher Robichaud.
© 2014 John Wiley & Sons, Inc. Published 2014 by John Wiley & Sons, Inc.

to answer in this chapter is the following: Is it ethical for a *D&D* character to summon a creature to do his or her bidding?

Mages and the Ethics of Summoning

Let's analyze the actions of mages first, as their relationships with animals often involve domination by powerful spells. Mages usually interact with animals in two ways: First, they can summon animals by using animal-summoning or monster-summoning spells. For example, a panicked or trapped mage could cast a spell, resulting in a number of animals appearing to fight by her side. Second, a mage can summon an animal to be her familiar. A familiar was once a normal animal that has been transformed into a magical beast with unique powers and abilities. Bats, cats, hawks, and rats are examples of common familiar companions. In contrast to animals summoned by animal- or monster-summoning spells, familiars are usually not involved in combat. Rather, they often play the role of a scout, servant, or simple companion.

Let's consider the example of a panicked or trapped mage summoning animals for aid in battle. Let's say that this mage is at a low level and only has the ability to call two rats. These two rats, presumably, were doing other things before the mage cast the summoning spell. They may have been building their nests or foraging for food. So we should ask here: Is it right for the mage to call them away from their self-directed tasks? Current work by animal ethicists can help us answer this question.

The contemporary philosopher Bernard Rollin argues that, for as long as we have been domesticating nonhuman others, we have had a social consensus ethic regarding the treatment of animals.[2] Roughly, this ethic forbade unnecessary, deliberate cruelty toward animals. Allusions to this ethic can be found in many historical documents, including the Bible and other religious texts. For example, in Deuteronomy it is written that "thou shalt not plow with an ox and a donkey together."[3] The reason behind this mandate is to lessen the suffering of animals, as an ox is much stronger than a donkey and the mismatch in strength will make the act of plowing painful for both. Another passage mandates that only a sharp knife should be used for animal butchering. Again, the sharp knife lessens pain. In addition, both Thomas Aquinas (1225–74) and Immanuel Kant (1724–1804) condemned animal cruelty because it could lead to the abuse of humans by humans.[4]

According to this "traditional animal ethic," largely accepted by humans before the advent of industrial agriculture, the simple act of summoning the two rats is not ethically wrong if it does not cause unnecessary suffering for the rats. Thus the mage could summon animals and still be acting ethically. However, in the above example the mage is essentially calling the rats into battle and also taking them away from tasks that may be necessary for their survival or wellbeing. Both of these acts could be understood as causing the animals unnecessary suffering and would, therefore, be wrong. Thus one could use the traditional animal ethic standpoint to argue both for and against the efficacy of summoning animals into battle.

While the traditional ethic could be used to both condone and argue against such treatment, other animal ethics may have a different assessment of the act of summoning animals into battle. For example, the contemporary philosopher Peter Singer uses a "utilitarian approach" to decide what is or is not the correct way to treat animals.[5] Specifically, he and other utilitarians argue that an ethical action is one that maximizes the greatest good for the greatest number of individuals. However, Singer's approach slightly differs because he argues that suffering should be the main ethical criterion that we need to take into account when deciding which action is the right one to take. Thus, for Singer, the action that brings about the least amount of suffering for the greatest number is the one that is ethical.

So let's say that the two rats died trying to save the mage's life. In this instance one could simplistically argue that calling the rats was ethically wrong because it caused more suffering (the death of *two* rats) than good (the survival of *one* mage). However, more weight might be given to the mage's life, because the mage may have many friends and family members who would all suffer because of her death. In that case, one could argue that it is ethical for the mage to summon the rats for help even if the rats die. It appears that we are at an impasse because the ethic could be used to argue that summoning is ethical and is not ethical. Let's turn to another animal ethicist for help.

The rights ethicist Tom Regan argues that animals have particular rights because they are subjects of a life, meaning that they seek to satisfy specific preferences and interests.[6] According to Regan, if an animal is a subject of a life, then we must respect its desire to pursue such goals. For example, the rats above may have preferences for building nests and walking along a particular pond at night. If this is the case, then the mage's act of summoning could be understood as a violation of the rats' basic right to pursue these interests. Thus, as long as the mage is forcefully summoning the rats, her act is unethical. It appears that two animal ethics can be used to condone summoning animals, while one forbids it.

Wizards and the Ethics of Familiars

What about familiars? While the above issue of summoning animals into battle may be problematic, surely having a furry or scale-covered familiar is acceptable? In this case, the mage grants special abilities to the animals and develops a long-term relationship with them. Sure, the animals may be separated from their home and companions during this process but they are well taken care of and usually not caused physical pain (this last point depends on the alignment of the mage, of course). In addition, in contrast to the rats we considered, these animals are generally not required to participate in combat. From the standpoint of the traditional ethic above, the act of taking and keeping a familiar appears because the animal is not caused needless suffering. However, other animal ethicists may not agree.

For example, let's return to Peter Singer's utilitarian animal ethic. If summoning a familiar means removing the animal from animal companions, who presumably will suffer because of this separation, then the act of taking a familiar may be unethical according to Singer. For example, if the mage takes a hawk that, prior to the summoning and subsequent magical transformation, has chicks and a mate, then the joy that the mage gains by taking the hawk as a familiar may be outweighed by the suffering caused by removing the hawk from its family. In addition, if the mage commands the familiar to do tasks that cause it more suffering than can be outweighed by benefits to the mage and others, then these actions would also be unethical according to Singer. However, if taking a familiar causes more overall good than suffering, then the action would be ethical. So which is it? Is the mage acting ethically or not? So far, as with the case of summoning animal aid in battle, we have votes for and against the positive ethical character of this particular action. Let's apply Regan's animal ethic to see if we can break the tie, so to speak.

Remember that, according to Tom Regan, animals have particular rights because they are subjects of a life. If this is the case, then Regan's ethic could be used to argue against obtaining a familiar. For example, the hawk may have a preference for mice and for flying the mountain passes of a particular region. If the mage denies the hawk these pursuits, then, according to this ethic, the mage would be acting unethically because she is not respecting the basic rights of the animal. In contrast to the traditional ethic, which would largely condone the use of animals as familiars, and the Singer's utilitarianism ethic, which could either condone or not condone such an action, Regan's ethic could be used to argue that such treatment is unethical.

Similarly, Rollin's "respect for *telos*" animal ethic mandates that we should follow the "maxim to respect *telos*" when deciding how to treat animals.[7] This maxim is, roughly, that if we have dealings with animals, we need to respect their needs and desires or their *telos*. This term was widely used by Aristotle (384–322 BCE) and has been highly influential throughout the history of philosophy. If you accept this ethic, then the mage's actions are again unethical because, through turning the familiar into a magical beast, the mage is not respecting the animal's *telos* because the she effectively changes that *telos* into something altogether different.

Animal Ethics and Character Alignment

We are again at an impasse as we are left with two ethics that could condone taking a familiar and two that deem the activity wrong. In addition, we are left with ethics that could be used to either condone or condemn summoning animals to battle, depending on the circumstances. So what is a *D&D* character to do in this situation? Well, that all depends on the character's alignment, of course. If your character is good then he or she would most likely take the above ethical arguments into consideration when deciding whether or not to take a familiar, and when deciding whether or not to summon animals to fight. Deciding whether or not it is the right thing to do may appear to be a difficult task, but no one said that playing a good character is easy. Often such characters are faced with difficult ethical dilemmas that have no clear cut answer. Hopefully, the ethics above can help you make wise and good choices.

In addition, identifying exactly which ethic your character is drawn to may create further character depth because it tells you something about your character's ethical makeup and problematizes the seemingly "easy" choice of doing good acts. For example, playing a good utilitarian mage will be a completely different experience than playing a good mage who wholeheartedly accepts Regan's rights-based ethic. While both have a good alignment, they will make strikingly different decisions in some situations.

In contrast to good characters, one with an evil alignment may ignore or even delight in knowing that his or her actions would be considered wrong by these measures. Think of the evil mage who summons magical beasts only to magically chain them and experiment upon them. Such characters would not be moved by ethical arguments. Finally, neutral characters may choose to take the above ethics into account or may choose not to. Such characters can take the middle ethical path and thus can stray in either direction. Mystra only knows what a chaotic neutral character would do in such a situation.

Druids and the Ethics of Summoning Animals

While wizards seem to have it particularly hard in the animal ethics department, other classes may have an easier time of determining the right way to treat animals. For example, both druids and rangers could potentially sidestep such ethical pitfalls. In *D&D*, a ranger can befriend animals and gain an animal companion (such as a bear, wolf, or falcon) after a particular level. Contrary to the relationship of wizards with nonhuman others, where they use the power of magic to force compliance and bind the animal to their will, rangers "befriend" nonhuman others. This implies that the relationship between ranger and animal is one of mutual respect that has been chosen by each party.

If this is the case, then each of the ethics above could be used to argue that such a relationship is ethical. For example, a person could argue that the ranger is respecting the rights of the animal to follow its own interests and is thus following Regan's ethic. In addition, a person could argue that she is respecting Rollin's maxim to respect *telos*. Finally, as she is simultaneously not causing the animal suffering (by separating it from its nonhuman companions) and benefiting from the animal's company, a person could use Singer's ethic to argue that this relationship is ethical. Thus it appears that it is relatively easy to determine whether or not the ability to form such relationships is ethical. This would also hold for druids, who can speak the language of animals, and call them when they are needed, as these animals come willingly.

Trouble in the Druid Grove

What if the animals die when they come to the aid of rangers or druids? Is the action still ethical? For example, what if a druid is attacked in the forest by group of bandits? Panicked, she calls out to the animals nearby for aid, and several birds, rabbits, and a boar come to help. In the process of defending the druid, several animals suffer injury and two of the rabbits die. In this instance, was it ethical for the druid to call upon the animals for help, even if giving this aid may mean their death?

According to Regan's ethic, the act of the druid calling for help is ethical because it did not violate the animals' right to pursue their own interests. If the rabbits made the choice to come to the druid's aid, then the druid should not be blamed for the consequences of their choices. However, according to Singer's ethic, this action may not be ethical, depending on the amount of suffering caused. If the suffering of the animals outweighs the good of saving the druid, then the druid would be wrong to save her skin at the expense of animal lives.

Again, the decision of the character to call for help will largely be determined by the alignment of the druid. A good druid or ranger may sacrifice her life to protect the animals of the forest, while an evil one would gladly sacrifice animal life for his own, no matter which action is right. However, it still holds that such relationships are less problematic than mage–animal relations.

Thus there appears to be a big difference between befriending animals and forcefully controlling animals in order to make them fight by your side. While the first skill set may be slightly problematic in some situations, the ability to form relationships and *ask* for help is not, by itself, problematic. In contrast, the mage, with her control of powerful magic, should be aware of the possibility that such power can be abused and cause the unnecessary suffering and death of nonhuman others. As Lord Acton wrote, "Power tends to corrupt, and absolute power corrupts absolutely."[8] It appears that this also holds in *Dungeons & Dragons*. Thus, when playing a character who can summon nonhuman animals, it may be wise to take the ethics into account when deciding what actions are best. At the very least, this will give you the opportunity to more fully develop a complex and interesting character.

Notes

1. Irene Pepperberg and Spencer K. Lynn, "Possible Levels of Animal Consciousness with Reference to Grey Parrots (Psittacus erithacus)," *American Zoologist* 40 (2000), pp. 893–901.
2. Bernard E. Rollin, *Farm Animal Welfare: Social, Biological, and Research Issues* (Ames: Iowa State University Press, 2003).
3. Deuteronomy 22: 10 (King James Bible).
4. Hugh Lafollette and Niall Shanks, *Brute Science: Dilemmas of Animal Experimentation* (New York: Routledge, 1996).
5. Peter Singer, *Animal Liberation* (New York: HarperCollins, 2002).
6. Tom Regan, *Animal Rights, Human Wrongs* (Oxford: Rowman & Littlefield, 2003).
7. B.E. Rollin, "On Telos and Genetic Engineering," in S.J. Armstrong and R.G. Botzler, eds., *The Animal Ethics Reader* (New York: Routledge, 2003), pp. 342–350.
8. The quote is from a "Letter to Bishop Mandell Creighton, April 5, 1887," published in *Historical Essays and Studies*, ed. J.N. Figgis and R.V. Laurence (London: Macmillan, 1907).

Part VI

DUNGEONS & DRAGONS OUT IN THE REAL WORLD

13

"Kill her, kill her! Oh God, I'm sorry!"
Spectating *Dungeons & Dragons*

Esther MacCallum-Stewart

Ten minutes into the YoGPoD episode 31 "*Dungeons & Dragons* Part 2*,*" the player Chris Lovasz, or Sips, decides he is going to passive-aggressively grief the rest of his party. "I'm just gonna make a camp, guys," he drawls, as the rest of the players interrogate the first quest-giver. As the game proceeds, Sips' camp-building deadlocks the adventure, as the players can't progress without him. In frustration, they methodically kill, threaten, and chase away any quest-givers that approach them. "Fuck me!" shouts the DM, as the party turn on the third consecutive NPC. "Do you guys not want to take any quests; ever?!" "Well, maybe if we kill him and loot his body, he'll have a piece of paper, or something," another player replies smugly. For the players, preventing the game from running and irritating the DM by thwarting his plans has become just as amusing as playing his dungeon, all of which is done with a longstanding, tongue-in-cheek understanding of how *D&D* ought to be played.

The YoGPoD podcast series was the forerunner for the highly successful Yogscast YouTube channel, which produces video-game walkthroughs, first looks, and reviews.[1] At its heart is the machinima adventure series *Shadow of Israphel*, recorded within the sandbox indie game *Minecraft* and charting the exploits of heroes and main hosts Xephos (Lewis Brindley) and Honeydew (Simon Lane). Like the podcasts, the series is light-hearted and highly intertextual, punctuated by fourth wall-breaking interjections about everything from soya milk to comments on the activity in the streets outside each player's window. The adventures of the duo are so popular that over 2 million people watch each episode, and their YouTube channel has over 1000 *Minecraft*-related videos, many of them played on customized adventure story maps made for them by fans. As Lewis Brindley explains, the adventure maps are a substitute for their *D&D* podcast episodes, adding visual context and enabling the acting out of more dramatic or spectacular events.

In 2011 Google financed 100 new YouTube channels in order to promote its subscription channels and encourage professional development within the platform. One of these, a channel named Geek and Sundry, was awarded to internet star and writer Felicia Day, well known for her webisode series *The Guild*, which charts the successes and failures of a fictitious MMO guild.[2] One of the most popular series on Geek and Sundry is called *Tabletop*, and shows geek celebrities and their friends playing board and tabletop role-playing games. Like the *Shadow of Israphel* series, each episode is watched by up to a million people.

Every year at PAX Prime (the Penny Arcade Exposition) in Seattle, a group of gamers assembles onstage to play *Dungeons & Dragons*. The group of nerd celebrities consists of Wil Wheaton, Jerry Holkins, Mike Krahulik, Scott Kurtz, and Chris Perkins. The session lasts about two hours. The 5000-seat venue is consistently filled to capacity, and queues to attend begin nearly two hours beforehand. In 2012 the session was used to showcase a beta version of the fifth edition *D&D* rules, testimony to both its popularity and its influence with other gamers.

The rise of these shows is at the center of geek chic, a growing subculture encompassing minority leisure activities such as comic book reading, gaming, role-playing, and science fiction/ fantasy literature. However, this is somewhat disingenuous. Though long-term gaming fans might be comforted to think that discussions about board-gaming, t-shirts with unicorns, or *Half-Life* mods are the next big thing, it is more likely that the transmedial nature of gaming fans and the texts that they consume allows them to communicate with each other more readily, thus creating a more widespread sense of shared identity. In addition, the interest for such activities has expanded, given that most 20–30-year-olds in the western world have grown up in environments where computer gaming is part of their childhood. Whether geek chic is cool is therefore debatable; more likely it is simply more accepted in mainstream culture. What is true, however, is that watching other people play *D&D* or games clearly derived from it seems to be becoming as interesting to people as actually playing for themselves.

This chapter examines this behavior. We will look at early adventure games based on *D&D*, asking why they avoid many aspects of the game, especially those that involve role-playing and moral decisions by players. We will then discuss how gamers now discover *D&D*, and why this is important in changing their under-standing of the game. Finally this brings us to the philosophical implication behind this discussion: why Pierre Levy's ideas about the digital age, virtual communities, and collective intelligence are so important for understanding how, and why this has happened.[3] To conclude we'll discuss the effects that this has on *D&D* players.

"Sixteen Diamonds' Worth of Dirt": Television and *Dungeons & Dragons*

The desire to re-create *Dungeons & Dragons* as visual enter-tainment is not new – *D&D* directly influenced a number of derivative television programs broadcast during the 1980s and 1990s – including *The Adventure Game* (1980–86), *Knightmare* (1987–94) and *The Crystal Maze* (1990–95). These programs allowed the game to be viewed by an audience as well as played. In these games, the dungeon format is taken literally, with players locked into each scenario, and forced to solve various physical, logistical, and verbal puzzles.

Although popular, and clearly derivative from *Dungeons & Dragons*, the programs were not intended to showcase the game but rather to provide versions which relied on a more familiar game/challenge show format for television audiences. This meant that players were contestants rather than characters, who took part in each game once and disappeared after their turn ended. They were either young professionals (*The Crystal Maze*), children (*Knightmare*), or children's celebrities (*The Adventure Game*). *The Crystal Maze* was clearly advertised as a management training exercise, with ties to its role-playing roots largely avoided. *Knightmare* and *The Adventure Game* were specifically made for children's television.

The programs demonstrate anxiety with adopting characters or specific roles. Players are adventurers or captives, but are not expected to adopt personae. The host of each show plays a type-cast Dungeon Master role, guiding each group around the maze or overseeing each quest, but their attitude is more game show host than NPC. In *The Crystal Maze*, the camp behavior of Richard O'Brien clearly embarrasses some contestants as he performs distracting capers or plays loudly on a harmonica during moments of tension. In *Knightmare*, the Dungeon Master Treguard often emphasizes his neutrality to players, preventing them from interacting with him or asking for clues. NPCs were, however, a feature. *The Adventure Game* is remembered for an array of eccentric characters including Uncle, an angry aspidistra plant, and various characters named after anagrams of the word Argond (the planet that all of the NPCs, whose natural form was a dragon, originated from). *The Adventure Game* has a science fiction theme and contestants are often shown playing early computer games or solving futuristic puzzles such as directing the remote-controlled Dogran through the computer game *Labyrinth*. Overall, these games contained characteristics such as quests and puzzles to solve, but role-play was solely to entertain, inform, or otherwise distract the contestant/viewer.

These games demonstrate the popularity of puzzle-solving and adventure games, but they point to issues with representing *D&D* to a mainstream audience. Each is extensively repurposed for television, with most aspects of tabletop play removed. Rolling dice, deliberation, role-play, map-making, moral choices, and combat are all gone. Jennifer Grouling Cover argues that this alteration is important because "While the new genre will have some commonalities with its antecedent, it will serve a different purpose for the audience."[4] In this case, necessary changes make the game more television-friendly, and they chime with established adventure game tropes already present in television programs.

It is not just the association with *D&D* and childishness that prevented television producers from replicating the game too closely. The "Satanic Panic" that surrounded role-playing games in the 1980s and 1990s had an obvious influence. Moral decisions and combat, the most problematized aspects of play, are not present. Players moderate their behavior – there is no swearing, frustration with puzzles is mild (of the "awww shucks!" variety), and players absolutely do not resort to violence or the arcane to solve issues. When Chris Searle makes the lightest of sexual innuendos in episode 3 of season 3 of *The Adventure Game* to Sandra Dickinson, "Could you pull my wire?", he immediately apologizes with a very English retraction "if you'll forgive my expression," and though contestants are allowed to vaporize their companions during the end puzzle, The Vortex, this is couched as "getting their own back" and done at the encouragement of a cheekily smiling Argond.

Overall, these games remake *D&D* as a puzzle-solving adventure to be watched rather than played. Fears that fantasy might corrupt children into deviant behavior mean that the imaginative nature of the game is removed in favor of a more practical approach. The viewer remains a spectator only. The early nature of these games also means that fan responses are absent. Although *The Adventure Show* sometimes contains a pre-recorded phone-in where children speculate on how to solve puzzles, these shows largely avoid such input. Overall, then, the sometimes complex moral decisions that have to be made in *D&D* games are avoided.

Legacies

T.L. Taylor and Emma Witkowski argue that when playing videogames the relationship between spectatorship and game-play needs to re-evaluated, because watching or otherwise commenting on games is a fundamental part of how we play and understand them. [5] Along with several other scholars, they argue that games are also consumed and enjoyed by spectators and non-participants, as well as those actively taking part. Supporting these arguments are the growing number of conventions hosting e-sport tournaments, online television channels showing gaming matches or first plays of recently released titles, e-sports channels on YouTube and TwitchTV, and the high levels of viewing for shows which present full walkthroughs or debriefs of games. If, as Taylor argues, e-sport events are increasingly regarded as a high-profile spectator activity in their own right,[6] it is also true that gaming – including role-playing games such as the first examples mentioned – is frequently watched as well as played. Amongst these spectated games are play-throughs of tabletop campaigns, stories using *D&D* precepts, and examples of role-play in games that lack their own narrative. It seems that there has been some sort of weather change over the last ten years. Making up stories and playing roles is not only fun, but it is fun to *watch*. It is therefore important to examine how players now approach the game, in order to understand why this might be the case.

Dungeons & Dragons was first published in 1974, forty years ago and more than enough time for a generation of players to grow up and introduce their own children to the game. The game is still thriving, new supplements and editions are regularly released, and many online communities are dedicated to playing, sharing, and reimagining the game. But when I first encountered *D&D* I only played it once, with my mother and younger brother. As DM, my mother gamely struggled through the solo adventure in the Red Box (1977), but had neither the time, nor the understanding to write more campaigns. The imaginative component of the game was just too alien. I clearly remember her inability to role-play the healing cleric NPC and her confusion at allocating treasure via a dice roll. My younger brother was more interested in removing the wax used on the dice, and redoing it with his crayons. These quickly became lost as a result, and despite my interest, the box was relegated to the back of the cupboard. Like Simon Lane of the Yogscast, it was not until I was well into my teenage years that I finally found a group of friends with whom to play the game properly.

These experiences are not uncommon. *D&D* is actually rather socially difficult to play – it requires a group of people (ideally about five or six) who can meet regularly, and who have similar understandings of what the game is about. As games scholars have pointed out, players do not play, or comprehend play, in the same way, and *D&D* games can vary wildly from purely spoken role-play to meticulously detailed movement on maps and charts.[7] Yet now, the influence of *D&D* has been so wide-reaching that it permeates gaming culture on every level,[8] making us aware of its core tropes without our having played it. As a child, I loved the television programs described above, and even applied to take part in *Knightmare*, but was unable to play *D&D* locally. For me, despite becoming an active larper, and taking part in many tabletop games over the years, it was MMOs that finally gave me the opportunity to take part in *D&D*-like games on a regular basis. I still love playing *D&D* and its tabletop derivatives, but I have also spent many memorable hours (days!) in Azeroth, Innistrad, Middle Earth, and Baldur's Gate. My experiences with *D&D* therefore have mixed influences; some of my knowledge comes from the vanilla text, but more comes from playing derivatives that remake elements of the game elsewhere.

Given these criteria, the age of the game, and the vast array of texts that emulate *D&D*, it is unsurprising that players are more likely to experience *D&D*-type play through other games and genres such as MMORPGs, card games like *Magic the Gathering*, and LARP events, videogames, or fiction. These media ape *D&D*'s structures, conventions, and tropes, yet it is very possible that their players are largely unaware of these origins. For them, *D&D* is simply another way to experience the rich diversity of geek culture, not the core text from which everything else derives. Crucially, although they may have a comprehensive under-standing of how *D&D* is expected to work, and may find it easy to understand if they do eventually start playing it, the game is not their primary frame of reference.

This feedback loop is one that is rarely considered, and it also has important philosophical ramifications, since it directly affects how players understand and interpret the game, what Pierre Levy calls their "collective intelligence." For example, the player may understand *D&D*'s archetypes through other modes of play such as the class system in *World of Warcraft*. When I introduce friends to role-playing games, they often use comparisons to understand the game on their own terms, for example by describing an NPC as a "quest-giver" or comparing statistical aspects with those within MMORPGs: "So, my magic points are like mana?" Usually, their interpretations are a simplified version of the more nuanced play available in a tabletop game (magic points have multiple uses, NPCs and their requests have more depth than simply asking players to kill twenty bears), and a direct result of experiencing more simplified *D&D* mechanics exhibited in derivative games.

As a result, publicly broadcast games often spend time explain-ing the game to the viewer, and providing them with intertextual references to aid their understanding. *D&D* is seen as existing amongst a corpus of games which all contain similar elements and can build creatively upon each other. The positive effect of this is that these players are not confined by the predetermined understandings or conventions that might exist within *D&D*.

For example, at the beginning of the PAX 2011 *D&D* session, "Acquisitions Incorporated: the Last Will and Testament of Jim Darkblade I,"[9] the players introduce themselves by recalling the previous game. Bards Paul and Strom provide additional sung commentary, warning the audience to "hold ye shit together," and expect an evening of "merriment and smack talk." Wil Wheaton (as Aoefel "Al" Elhromane) reminds everyone that in 2009, the group "split the party," causing his fae character to drown in a pool of acid. Scott Kurtz cautions the audience not to heckle because "being funny is for us," and as stage hands bring on a large table and the group take large folders from its drawers, Jerry Krahulik jokes with them, "Is this not how it happens at your house?" This introduction serves several purposes. It introduces the temperament of the players and their characters. It lays out social rules for the game (namely, that the audience should remain passive spectators during the session but also expect excitement, unusual situations, and humor), and it establishes the players as familiar with the gaming discourses and behavior required. The introduction also places the players in the position of experts, representative of both gamer and gameplay.

The players also take care to provide explanations that might not otherwise be present. Collectively their characters represent the most familiar classes and races of *D&D*, and both the DM and the players talk through their actions, and what meaning these have in terms of gameplay, as they take each step in the game. Thus, Acquisitions Incorporated is as much about teaching players to play – probably why the game is sponsored by Wizards of the Coast – as it is about the entertainment occurring on the stage. The participants carefully regulate their behavior to make this possible, so that as a spectated event, the game requires some familiarity with geek culture and gaming, but not an in-depth knowledge of *Dungeons & Dragons*. Intertextual references bolster this – at one point during the combat encounter, Kurtz comments "I've done this encounter before in Utgarde Keep. I'm going to do this one just the same – with half my attention on Netflix!" Utgarde Keep is a well-known instance (dungeon) in *World of Warcraft*, with a similar encounter to the one being experienced in the game (various stone animals come to life and attack the players), and is also known for being rather easy. Netflix is a television service which can be watched online. These two references – both from geek culture rather than *D&D* itself – instantly give the audience a comparative framework with which to appreciate the action and to revel in their own intertextual sharing, reinforcing the sense of belonging (or "communitas") between stage and audience.

These spectated games allow events which may seem relatively mundane to experienced players to be discovered as original content by others. This also encourages both reimagination and subversion, with players approaching the text from new directions and without preconceptions, and trying to surprise each other with new modes of play taken from more current, related texts. It also demonstrates a type of sharing typical of virtual spaces.

"Don't blow the Daily" Learning 2 Play

Pierre Levy understands the cybertext era as one in which collective endeavor will lead to new, self-regulated virtual spaces. Although his work is philosophical, it also has sociological and anthropological implications, which means that it can be applied in very practical terms to popular culture. Levy argues that post-2000, we have entered an age in which knowledge is shared differently, leading in turn to new ways of understanding how we form communities. His writing is commonly used in studies of new media and popular culture as a way of understanding the changes that have come about as a result of the virtual revolution. Within cyberspaces, Levy sees knowledge as the sum of many different voices, what he calls "collective intelligence." These voices are often spontaneously formed around need or shared interest rather than duty, and although collective intelligence, and more recent agile thinking can be applied in managerial ways, these groups are rarely seen as working within the confines of official bodies. Instead, they are more like the communities who create adventure maps in *Minecraft* for the Yogscast to play, or the people who send interesting links to Felicia Day's weekly *Flog*: experts contributing their knowledge to a collective whole. Most of these people have one very specific area of expertise, but they share it openly to create a larger pool of composite ideas. Thus, virtual spaces and communities vary according to who is using them, and when and why they are being used. They can also change very rapidly as interest shifts to new areas or expertise is needed elsewhere, and are seen as egalitarian, since they follow the principles that information wants to be (and is) free.

Levy is cited extensively by researchers of online communities.[10] Henry Jenkins sees the textual poaching and transmedial behavior of fans who appropriate what they need online and change it for their own ends as an increasingly commonplace activity. James Newman uses the idea to discuss how online groups form a sense of "communitas" which helps them create a sense of belonging.[11] Both of these activities can be seen in the examples I have given, as fans become more visible, share their experience with others, and help to pass this information on via virtual and subcultural means such as geek chic products. Collective intelligence also allows the sharing of prior ideas in new contexts – in this case, the use of *D&D* tropes employed in current media to explain how traditional *D&D* can be played.

The Yogscast, PAX games, and Tabletop all present to the audience an idealized session of *D&D* or other role-playing/ geek prowess. Because the session is played by people known for their affection for, and ability to satirize, geek culture, it is expected to be humorous and intelligent. There is an element of envy, "What if I could play games as epic as this?" but also identification, largely created by the dice rolls or unexpected events: "That has totally happened to me!" The games also showcase positive relationships – affectionate but teasing, occasionally crude, but never personal or mean. The games educate the observer socially as well as ludically. So for example it's okay to make jokes about the other player characters, or mistakes made in the past, but overly sexualizing the "busty" (previously misread as "bushy") female NPC in the PAX game is specifically avoided, and the Yogscast caution each other when their NPCs' stereotypes go too far, or swearing becomes excessive. Overall, the games are entertaining to watch, but are also instructional.

When Brindley and Lane started the *Shadow of Israphel* series, they had similar objectives in mind but also wanted to spice up the more mundane "how to" explanation of the games. Their attempts to enliven a relatively straightforward walkthrough of *Minecraft* resulted in a creative exploration of the text that allowed them to dip in and out of a role-played narrative. Sometimes, Xephos and Honeydew are brave adventurers exploring strange realms and interacting with a series of eccentric characters. Other times, they are simply two players chatting about their everyday lives while they build a base. They are, however, players whom the audience wish to emulate. Their obvious friendship is coupled with a dry sense of humor, and their surprised responses to each challenge, which can involve screaming with terror, crying out in anger, or generally yelling in frustration at the chaotic goings on around them, endorse a type of buddylect[12] that not only endears them to an audience, but also provides an idealized model of gameplay. The videos appear spontaneous, although in reality they are meticulously crafted and the maps take weeks to build. The conversations between the two are uncontrived, but nevertheless have taken years of cementing, and sometimes careful editing (especially to avoid mundane aspects like talking over each other, too loudly or out of synch with video footage) in order to perfect.

Levy's argument is that online communities learn and share from each other according to need, not official constraints. For *Dungeons & Dragons*, this means teaching players acceptable ways to play a game they might understand in theory, but not in practice, by showing them what to do rather than trolling through the rulebooks. It also means appropriating the parts of *D&D* that have become more commonly known in gaming culture, and showing audiences how, and why these apply to the game. All three groups moderate their performances accordingly – they avoid pejorative comments and they make deliberate attempts to be witty, as well as spending time on explanation or visualization. As a result, all three groups are elevated within the community to celebrity status because they are seen as representative of the community's best aspects. They also epitomize Levy's argument that the understanding of a single text must and will shift in accordance with the needs of a group who wish to understand it under new terms.

Notes

1. Lewis Brindley and Simon Lane, *The YoGPoD* (2009–), available on iTunes; Lewis Brindley and Simon Lane, *The Yogscast* (2009–), available on YouTube at http://www.youtube.com/user/Blue Xephos; accessed March 24, 2014.
2. Felicia Day, Geek and Sundry (2012–), available on YouTube at http://www.youtube.com/user/geekandsundry; accessed March 24, 2014.
3. See Pierre Levy, *Collective Intelligence: Mankind's Emerging World in Cyberspace* (New York: Basic Books, 1999).
4. Jennifer Grouling Cover, *The Creation of Narrative in Tabletop Role-Playing Games* (Jefferson, NC: McFarland, 2010), p. 50.
5. T.L. Taylor and Emma Witkowski, "This Is How We Play It: What a Mega-LAN Can Teach about Games," paper given at the Foundations of Digital Games Conference, Monterey, CA, 2010, available at http://tltaylor.com/wp-content/uploads/2010/06/TaylorWitkowski-ThisIsHowWePlayIt.pdf; accessed March 24, 2014.
6. T.L. Taylor, *Raising the Stakes: E-Sports and the Professionalization of Computer Gaming* (Cambridge, MA: MIT Press, 2012).
7. See for example James Newman, *Playing with Videogames* (London: Routledge, 2008); Garry Crawford, *Video Gamers* (London: Routledge, 2011); and Helen Thornham, *Ethnographies of the Videogame: Gender, Narrative and Praxis* (London: Routledge, 2011).
8. Mark Barrowcliff, *The Elfish Gene* (London: Pan Macmillan, 2008); Ethan Gilsdorf, *Fantasy Freaks and Gaming Geeks: An Epic Quest for Reality among Role Players, Online Gamers and other Dwellers of Imaginary Realms* (New York: Globe Pequot Press, 2009); and Grouling Cover, *The Creation of Narrative in Tabletop Role-Playing Games*.
9. Wizards of the Coast and Penny Arcade, "The Last Will and Testament of Jim Darkmagic I," Live *Dungeons & Dragons* game played at PAX 2011, available at http://www.wizards.com/dnd/article.aspx?x=dnd/4news/paxgame; accessed March 24, 2014.
10. Matt Barton, *Dungeons and Desktops: The History of Computer Role-Playing Games* (Massachusetts: A.K. Peters, 2008).

11. Most specifically Henry Jenkins, *Textual Poachers: Television Fans and Participatory Culture* (New York: Routledge, 1992) and *Convergence Culture: Where Old and New Media Collide* (New York: New York University Press, 2006), and James Newman, *Playing with Videogames* (London: Routledge, 2008).

12. Astrid Ensslin, *The Language of Gaming* (London: Palgrave Macmillan, 2011).

Berserker in a Skirt
Sex and Gender in *Dungeons & Dragons*

Shannon M. Mussett

As a young girl, I always chose to play the role of druid in *D&D* because that class allowed for the perfect blend of magic, the association with animals and the healing arts, and just enough weaponry so as not to be as much of a sissy as a magic user. In short, it felt girlie enough and yet tough enough that my older brother would still let me play with him and his friends. As I rediscovered *D&D* as an adult, I found myself more drawn to being a fighter – the barbarian class in particular – even entertaining the madness of the berserker from time to time. At a certain point, I had to ask myself why I had so radically abandoned what I perceived to be the gentle docility of a druid in favor of the bashing ethos of the fighter. I determined that my education and writing in feminist philosophy enabled me to embody a far more dangerous and physical fantasy than I would have previously allowed myself. Surprisingly, *D&D*, as the quintessential RPG, pointed me to something about the nature of gender that academic discussions on the topic could not quite capture, namely, that gender identities and gender roles are far more fluid than we realize in our daily exchanges. Although *D&D* on the whole does not actively promote the notion of

Dungeons & Dragons and Philosophy: Read and Gain Advantage on All Wisdom Checks, First Edition. Edited by Christopher Robichaud.
© 2014 John Wiley & Sons, Inc. Published 2014 by John Wiley & Sons, Inc.

gender flexibility, I believe that the deeply imaginative structure of the game can allow for players to explore the intricacies of gender and sexuality in creative and potentially radical ways. Where better than in a dungeon of the mind, surrounded by friends pretending to be elves and dwarves, to play with this idea?

Sex and Gender

Although it often comes as a surprise to find that some people either have played *D&D* in their younger years or continue to play well into their adult years, the surprise always seems greater when the player in question is a woman. It is no secret that most who play tend to be boys and men, and there is little doubt that the world of *Dungeons & Dragons* is largely geared toward a masculine, rather than a feminine, fantasy. One would be hard pressed to argue that cartoonishly large breasts and skin-tight leather skirts really allow for dexterous swordplay or quick get-aways. And yet, for some of us who play, there seems to be something liberating in taking on the roles of both male and female characters in the world of *D&D*. One of the first choices that one makes in rolling a character is the sex: male or female. Sure it's fun to decide whether or not one will play a bard or a druid, but how about the foundational decision to be a man or a woman? Many of us make this choice automatically (usually playing our own sex). But it is fascinating that in a game of sup-posed brutally physical adventuring, it doesn't really *matter*, as far as the success of the character, *which* sex one chooses to be.

As Shelly Mazzanoble notes, "One of the coolest things about *D&D* is gender equality. As in real life, whichever gender you choose to play is a matter of personal preference but unlike the real world, female and male characters are equals."[1] Here we see a critical, if often challenged, distinction between sex and gender that lies at the heart of feminist scholarship. Typically, one's sex is tied to biological or physiological descriptions – what organs one has, or what hormones are coursing through one's body. We tend to believe that biological sex is determined by physical forces that are largely beyond our power to alter – at least without varying degrees of medical intervention. One's gender however, depends on whether or not one exhibits masculine or feminine behaviors and traits. In other words, my gender is a matter of whether or not I *act* like a boy or a girl. I can play a little bit more with gender insofar as I entertain different roles, but we also tend to think unreflectively that gender is somewhat fixed as well. If this distinction can be upheld (and some wisely argue that the distinction is altogether problematic) then the question arises: is one's biological sex a *cause* of one's gender or are they entirely separate? Put differently, are the mannerisms of masculinity and femininity tethered to whether or not one has ovaries or testes or are they only loosely connected? Can we even inquire into the differences between biological sex and socially constructed gender from within language, which often imports assumptions about these terms by the very rules of its execution?

Simone de Beauvoir (1908–86), acutely aware of the problems of asking about women from within a historical discourse dominated by the male point of view, noted in 1949: "If I want to define myself, I first have to say, 'I am a woman'; all other assertions will arise from this basic truth. A man never begins by positing himself as an individual of a certain sex: that he is a man is obvious."[2] As Beauvoir points out, language favors men insofar as "man" is often assumed to be "human" (think of our use of "mankind" to mean all human beings, for example). If I am a woman, I have to first make it clear that I am a woman when I talk about myself – as if being a woman is a special class of human being and being a man is not.

And yet the differences between human beings based on sex *are* important, both socially and philosophically. As contemporary philosopher Luce Irigaray (1930–) claims, "sexual difference is one of the major philosophical issues, if not the issue, of our age."[3] The first thing we say about a child when it is born is: "It's a boy!" or "It's a girl!" In other words, the first distinction we draw between human beings is a distinction based on sex, so sexual difference must be pretty important for philosophy even

if it's not immediately so in *D&D*. But this fundamental distinction is so central as to be almost invisible to us, which is why
philosophers such as Irigaray believe it may be the defining issue
of our age. In *D&D* (as in mundane life) the issue of sex is
relatively concealed even among the explosion of images of male
and female characters and monsters. Philosophy can make this
invisible issue more visible by critically examining it in language,
and role-playing games such as *D&D* can allow us to explore
these structures by actively engaging them in imaginary
campaigns – thus effectively putting theory into practice.

Although I earlier mentioned that the first choice we make in
rolling a character is their sex, this is actually nowhere made
explicit in the rules of the game. Take a look at the character-
generation guidelines in various editions of the *Player's
Handbook*: the second edition (1989), the 3.5 edition (2003),
and the fourth edition (2008). In all of them, we are told that
the first deliberate decision that we make after we have taken
our chances with the random role of the die is to choose our
race and class. Certainly this makes sense – you need to know
whether or not the "genes" of your rolls allow you to be a
dwarf fighter or a half-elf thief – but why isn't the decision
about sex primary to all of it? The writers of each *Handbook*
have increasingly become more sensitive to the issues of gender
bias by using "he or she" or "you" instead of "he" and by using
females as examples of characters as well as males with almost
as much frequency.[4] Such sensitivity, as well as the fact that sex
does not affect one's success in almost any imaginable campaign,
is laudable. But yet why wouldn't the choice of sex – and gender –
be just as central to the fun of character creation as one's race
and class?

Gender Games

As Beauvoir notably asserts in *The Second Sex*, "One is not
born, but rather becomes, woman."[5] By this, she means that
there is nothing (or at least very little) that causes a biological

female to become the social construction of a "woman." Rather, women are made through multiple forces that can be examined through philosophy, anthropology, sociology, history, mythology, literature, and so on. If she were to take a side on the sex/gender distinction, Beauvoir would certainly favor the gender side – there is no feminine essence that can be linked to biology or physiology. She is also an existentialist philosopher, which means that she advocates a conception of radical freedom where we *choose* who we are because there is no such thing as a set human nature determining our actions. Once we apply this idea of existential freedom to the question of gender, we see that we can actually *choose* our gender, rather than be held captive by it. And how exciting is this revelation in terms of *D&D*?

Think of it this way – *D&D* liberates us from the limitations of our sex by making male and female characters equal in terms of abilities. Therefore, there is no *disadvantage* to playing a man or a woman in any of the races or classes. Taking it a step further, since there is no inherent limitation to a character's sex, this means that men and women (and even better, boys and girls) who play the game can play their own sex or the other sex with full freedom from unnecessary constraint. And to go one step further than that, choosing the sex of the character – whether it is your own or the opposite – does not tie one to a particular set of gender traits.[6] The shyest of men can be the most outspoken of wizards, the most honest girl can play the most unscrupulous rogue, and the pacifist woman can don full armor and fly into a berserker rage on a group of bugbears ambushing her adventuring party because, after all, bugbears are her species enemy and she just can't help herself when they are around.

Fantasy and Imagination as Vehicles for Social Change

So if we accept the common feminist presupposition that gender is not necessarily tied to our biological sex (and even if it were, good luck getting past our cultural codes and gendered language norms to somehow gain access to it), then we can see some of the revolutionary power of envisioning different gender norms. That's right: *D&D* can actually bring about feminist social change. To explore this point, let's think about what the imagination is and how it functions on a social level. One key method employed by any dominant and dominating system of power (political, social, pedagogical, you name it) is to curtail any collective change that might threaten its claims to legitimacy. One of the best ways to do this is to limit the ability of those under its power to imagine a different kind of reality. For example, if I want to convince slaves that their state is one imposed by nature (that they are slaves essentially and not by mere convention) then I actively discourage or disallow stories, poems, criticism, and religious ideas that might cause them to imagine that their lot could be otherwise. To limit the imagination is to limit critical thinking in the most brutal way, which keeps people subjected and afraid of change. *D&D*, on the other hand, requires that to play the game well, one *has* to use the imagination actively. One has to invent a character – with a past history, present situation, and future goals – place him or her in a totally fantastic fictional world with other imaginary characters, and try to solve problems that may be unreal (I mean, how many times does one have to combat a gelatinous cube at the office?) but which still require using problem-solving and creativity.

The first step in all of this is, of course, to imagine oneself as a completely different person – but a different person who yet relies 100 percent on the mind and experiences of the creator. We find this mantra repeated in various editions of the *Player's Handbook*. In the second edition we are told: "The character you create is your alter ego in the fantasy realm of this game, a make-believe person who is under your control and through whom you vicariously explore the world the Dungeon Master (DM) has created."[7] In the fourth edition we are called to "take a minute to imagine your character. Think about the kind of hero you want your character to be. Your character exists in your imagination – all the game statistics do is help you determine what your character can do in the game."[8] In other words, the entire game is there merely to support your own creative vision, not to dictate it to you or to play it for you. Such a core component of the game emphasizes the allure of transforming oneself imaginatively into something that one feels utterly unable or at least discouraged to do in mundane life.

For example, this transformative appeal can be seen in spellcasting. One of the key draws for classes like rangers, druids, and bards, and *the* attraction of the wizard class, is the ability to cast spells – many of which involve the alteration of the character into some other form. The 1st-level bard spell, *disguise self* and the 2nd-level *alter self* are obvious in this regard, as is the shared cleric, druid, and wizard spell, *shapechange*. One of the most popular schools of magic, the Illusion School, uses spells to "deceive the senses or minds of others. They cause people to see things that are not there, not see things that are there, hear phantom noises, or remember things that never happened."[9] Even more relevant, perhaps, is the Transmutation School, wherein one can "change the properties of some creature, thing or condition,"[10] thus allowing the spell caster to do amazing things such as *enlarge* or *reduce person, alter self*, or even *polymorph*. And yet in all of these spells, whether one is changing one's appearance to look like someone else, to appear as an animal, or to appear different in size, there is no real desire or necessity to change into the other sex. In part, this is because, as noted above, there is no noticeable disadvantage to playing one sex or the other in the world of *D&D*. And whereas one could envision a situation wherein a bard may need to change into the other sex to talk up the owner of a tavern for some information, sex and gender remain relatively invisible against the backdrop of swordplay and thievery that draws us all to the game in the first place. But this may be a missed opportunity for game players to use their imaginative power to conceive of different realities that could spill over positively into their daily lives.

Let us return to the power of this largely invisible issue of sex/gender from the larger perspective of feminism. Two feminists are helpful in this endeavor: Luce Irigaray (mentioned above) and contemporary philosopher Judith Butler (1956–), albeit for different reasons. Irigaray believes that sexual difference, as the key issue of our age for philosophy, has been made invisible by the way in which the male perspective (in language primarily, but also how this perspective bleeds into culture, politics, literature, and any other major human endeavor – even games!) dominates how we think about others and ourselves. This leads to a kind of *sameness*, wherein we reproduce the same ideas, arguments, and patterns instead of allowing for different – specifically feminine – perspectives to emerge. As a result, women are forced to "masquerade" at being what men think they should be – to wear a kind of "girl" costume so that men will desire them. Rather than masquerading a fake notion of femininity in order to be desired by men (which really just fails for both men and women), Irigaray advocates the strategy of "mimicry" where women take on and exaggerate the cultural norms of femininity in order to uncover how they work to situate women in oppressive constructs. She tells women to "come out [of] their [men's] language. Try to go back through the names they've given you"[11] in order to reveal the bias and artificiality of linguistic structures. Once we recognize the masculine biases inherent in language, we see how even our imaginations are fixated on a particularly masculine desire and orientation. This is an issue that is important in the fantasy world of *D&D*, which evokes a certain kind of masculine desire.

Using elements of psychoanalysis from Sigmund Freud (1856–1939) and Jacques Lacan (1901–81), Irigaray argues that we have an imaginary body that is largely imbued with fantasy. In other words, my body, as imagined by my mind (or ego) is *not* an objective representation of how it actually *is* (which is impossible to access) but is an artificial creation resulting from my entrance into language and society with others. What language says about bodies – male and female – within a cultural framework largely determines what we imagine our bodies are, what they can do, and what they look like. The imaginary body is an inevitable result of our entrance into culture for Irigaray. As such, there are a lot of pitfalls that can result from *distorted* imaginary bodies (eating disorders, for example, emerge out a problematic self-perception of the imaginary body) but also a lot of promise for what we can do when we actively change our perceptions through imaginative exploration. If I realize that my view of my body is largely imaginary, and I free my imagination from harmful self-representations by exaggerating and miming them – essentially making fun of them – then I can conceive of totally new ways to be in the world. In other words, by using mimicry, I can see how problematic many formulations of gender are and thus be motivated to reject them if they are harmful to others and myself. And where better can we see this mechanism than in the world of *D&D*? Open up to any page in any manual and you will find the imaginary body writ large. Males and females from a variety of races with impossible beauty, grace, strength, fabulous clothing, and weaponry that would make a medieval knight swoon.

Obviously there is something a little annoying about the buxom women who are supposed to be able to fight all gussied up. One cannot really deny that these images, like their comic book counterparts, are the *male* imaginary run amok. But once we see that, we can begin to play around with these images. Both men and women players are free to choose whatever sex they want to play and then on top of that, whatever gender as well. If we can stretch our minds beyond the limitations of our own imaginary bodies, as well as the bodies depicted in the books and miniatures, just think of where we can go to liberate ourselves from sexist representations. Are you a scrawny, awkward girl with braces? Why not play a 6-foot 4-inch male paladin? Are you a stout 40-year-old dockworker? Why not play a lithe, 250-year-old, female elf paladin? Are you young? Play an ancient wizard on the way out of this life! Are you straight? Play a bisexual, halfling druid on a revenge mission! The only question to ask yourself is: why *not*?

Berserker in a Skirt

One thing that I have come to realize is that my own game play has increasingly become less an extension of what I think I could realistically do (as a young girl, I figured a skinny, animal-loving druid was what I could actually pull off if *D&D* were "real") and more a way for me to strain myself into imagining sex and gender far beyond my comfort zone. This led me to realize that different players therefore can either magnify their own self-image (or imaginary body) whereas others can try to totally alter it through character construction.

Judith Butler can help us think this through. At the end of *Gender Trouble,* a work that challenges the very idea of a *natural* sex, Butler turns to a discussion of drag and cross-dressing. What is it, she asks, that is so captivating in the performance of drag? Whether in a show on a cruise ship or mildly exaggerated butch/femme identities in the gay and lesbian communities, drag reveals something that otherwise remains largely concealed from us. Namely, drag illustrates that gender itself is performative. That's right – gender doesn't express some kind of inner gender core, but rather shows us that all of our gendered mannerisms are a performance that gives us only the *illusion* that we have some kind of masculine or feminine essence. It's not like any girl (or boy) naturally takes to a pair of high heels – one has to *train* oneself to walk in them through many repetitions, thus retroactively creating the idea that women can and should wear high heels because they have some kind of feminine essence. This gendered nature is like a *glamor* spell that gets cast on us at a very early age. But it is really only retroactively produced by the habitual repetition of various gender performances (like performing walking in high heels) and in no way *expresses* some kind of human nature.

These performances are not benign according to Butler. They produce social and political ramifications wherein we are kept in line, monitored, and controlled without anyone having to do anything because we do it to *ourselves*: Am I acting masculine enough as I am walking down the hallway? Is it feminine for me to eat like that? What if I don't really care who wins the big game – do I still have to fake it? If I want to cut my hair short will everyone think I am lesbian (whether or not I am)? So much energy trying to live up to the fantasy of a true gender! And guess what? Everyone fails to do so. What is so entertaining and often funny about drag is that it highlights the performative nature of gender identity – "*in imitating gender, drag implicitly reveals the imitative structure of gender itself.*"[12] Drag shows us that there is no original gender core because the parody of a man, for example, wearing lavish makeup, sequins, and high-heeled boots magnifies the silliness of many women doing the same on their way to work.

What happens when we open the pages of the *Player's Handbook*? Well I don't know about you, but if those Eladrin on page 38 of the fourth edition *Handbook* aren't in drag, then I don't know who is. And isn't that part of what makes the game so enjoyable? I may be embarrassed by my desire to wear shining velvet and lace robes in reality (since Stevie Nicks was probably the last one who was able to pull off that look), but once I become Archimodar, the 4th-level Transmutor Mage, I can relish in the swishing of the luxurious fabric as I cast *magic missile* on the kobold swarm. And as for myself, I may be nervous directly confronting (often male) authority at my day job, dressed in my TJ Maxx finest casual business-wear, but once I become Raya the Barbarian, low on charisma (and thus known to smell a little off-putting to her fellow adventurers) but high in ass-kicking with a war hammer, I can fly into a rage that lasts five rounds. And boy, does that feel awesome.

Liberation and Laughter

Do I want to be a large, smelly barbarian in "real" life? Good God no, how *unfeminine*. But when I play one in *D&D*, I realize that femininity is itself a construct – both in my own world and in the world populated by dungeons and dragons. And this realization allows me to laugh at the unrealistic gender expectations we all try and fail to embody. As Butler points out, "the loss of the sense of 'the normal,' however, can be its own occasion for laughter, especially when 'the normal,' the original' is revealed to be a copy, and an inevitably failed one, an ideal that no one *can* embody. In this sense, laughter emerges in the realization that all along the original was derived."[13] Do we laugh at drag queens in the Pride Parade? You bet. And do we laugh at ourselves, painstakingly painting our minis as if these avatars were really copies of the original *us* transported to Toxer, the mining town at the foot of the Slippery Mountains? Of course. And do people who don't play RPGs laugh at us because we play *D&D*? Well, obviously. But we have the last laugh, because in role-playing all these male and female characters performing nearly infinite variations of masculinity and femininity, we see something that many people go through life never realizing – gaming our genders in the world of fantasy, means we can game them in our daily lives – and *that*, is what liberation is all about. So, who's laughing now?

Acknowledgments

I would like to thank the Utah Valley University Philosophy Club for their feedback on this paper, especially Kris McLain, Ray Mucillo, John Christensen, and Richard Blackburn. I would also like to thank C. Thi Nguyen and Mike Shaw for their comments on earlier drafts, and Matt Horn for being such a great Dungeon Master.

Notes

1. Shelly Mazzanoble, *Confessions of a Part-Time Sorceress: A Girl's Guide to the Dungeons & Dragons Game* (Renton, WA: Wizards of the Coast, 2007), p. 32.
2. Simone de Beauvoir, *The Second Sex*, trans. Constance Borde and Sheila Malovany-Chevallier (New York: Alfred A. Knopf, 2010), p. 5.

3. Luce Irigaray, *An Ethics of Sexual Difference*, trans. Carolyn Burke and Gillian C. Gill (Ithaca, NY: Cornell University Press, 1993), p. 5.

4. The makers of *D&D* have become more aware of the use of gender-exclusive language over time. For example, in the second edition they claim that the male pronoun is used throughout the book not to discourage women from playing, but because "centuries of use have neutered the male pronoun. In written material it is clear, concise, and familiar. Nothing else is" (Steve Winter and Jon Pickens, *Advanced Dungeons & Dragons, Player's Handbook for the AD&D Game*, 2nd edn. [Lake Geneva, WI: Tactical Studies Rules, 1996], p. 9). By the time of the fourth edition, this idea of male pronouns representing all people has been largely abandoned, and rightly so.

5. Beauvoir, *The Second Sex*, p. 283.

6. Special settings do entertain the relationship between sex and gender such as we find with the sexless Warforged in the Eberron campaign that can actually choose their gender.

7. *Player's Handbook*, 2nd edn., p. 18.

8. Rob Heinsoo, Andy Collins, and James Wyatt, *Player's Handbook: Arcane, Divine and Martial Heroes*, vol. 4 (Renton, WA: Wizards of the Coast, 2008), p. 14.

9. Monte Cook, Jonathan Tweet, and Skip Williams, *Dungeons & Dragons Player's Handbook*, 3.5 edn. (Renton, WA: Wizards of the Coast, 2003), p. 173.

10. Ibid., p. 174.

11. Luce Irigaray, *The Sex Which Is Not One*, trans. Catherine Porter (Ithaca, NY: Cornell University Press, 1985), p. 205.

12. Judith Butler, *Gender Trouble: Feminism and the Subversion of Identity* (New York: Routledge, 1990), p. 137.

13. Ibid., p. 139.

15

"Others play at dice"[1]
Friendship and *Dungeons & Dragons*

Jeffery L. Nicholas

D&D gamers exemplify Aristotle's claim that "no one would want to live without friends" (1155a5). The popular view is that a gamer is a loner or maybe even a loser, someone without friends, who maybe spends his time in a room alone or, if he has managed to find other losers like himself, in his mom's basement until he's 40, unemployed, and still a virgin. Movies like *Saving Silverman* or *Shaun of the Dead* play with this stereotype, sometimes reinforcing it and at other times resisting it. Yet gamers in fact value friendship highly. One might even see gaming as an attempt to find friends and build that political community of which Aristotle says friendship is the root. The really interesting thing about gamers is that, as they play *Dungeons & Dragons*, they at one and the same time build bonds between their characters and between each other as players. The trajectory of these bonds often mirrors the trajectory of friendships we find in epic fantasy literature where the characters, at first suspicious of each other, in the end have developed true friendships and established peaceful kingdoms where chaos had reigned before. As we'll see, Aristotle's philosophy of friendship can help us to understand this development.

Dungeons & Dragons and Philosophy: Read and Gain Advantage on All Wisdom Checks, First Edition. Edited by Christopher Robichaud.
© 2014 John Wiley & Sons, Inc. Published 2014 by John Wiley & Sons, Inc.

WANTED

New In Town and Looking to Join a Game

(*Please*)

Many of us begin playing *Dungeons & Dragons* when we are teenagers. We might chance upon it when someone in our school invites us to play, or we might seek it out because older siblings have played it, or, today, maybe our parents have been playing it since we were infants. Later, when we go to college or move on in life, we seek out others to game. Why do we go through such trouble trying to find other *D&D* players? Are we that desperate, and won't we ever grow up? As an academic, I've moved around a bit chasing an MA, then a PhD, and finally a job. Each time I've sought and found a *D&D* group, and each time some of the people I gamed with became good friends. Some even became true friends.

If you've moved around a lot, you know the routine. You come to a new city, you troll Craigslist, hunt on Wizards of the West Coast boards, hang out at the closest gaming store, posting signs explaining what a great gamer you are and that you're looking for a group. You're even willing to be Dungeon Master if others take turns as well. How quickly you find a group varies: a week, several months, maybe a year or two. It's much easier to find groups in college and grad school than it is outside of college, but eventually you find some group.

Initially, you meet the other players wondering who they are, what kind of gaming they like – hack-n-slash or more role-playing, or a good mixture. Such meetings mirror the way we meet others in a variety of situations – colleagues at work, people at church, a stranger at a party to which we've been invited. These initial meetings comprise a form of friendship that Aristotle calls friends of utility. Friendships of utility are often brief and motivated by some extrinsic good. They easily develop conflict, and do not add much to the search for virtue or flourishing. Yet they are necessary in life.

A friendship of utility is just what it sounds like. Two or more people come together to gain some advantage from each other. Aristotle calls this a friendship, though the least like true friendship. Each person in the friendship wishes something good for himself and for the others in the agreement, and some equality grounds the friendship. In the case of a *D&D* gaming group, you meet some other gamers to enjoy a game of *Dungeons & Dragons*. This group does not yet amount to a friendship of pleasure, because, initially, the members are not sure if they will in fact find any pleasure in the company of the other players.

Further, "accusations and blame arise in the friendship based on utility, either in it alone or in it especially with good reason" (1162b5–6). Until your gaming group has gamed together for a while and established house rules and some routine, players might squabble with each other or with the Dungeon Master. "How did he get an 18 strength?" or "The die was cocked!" The DM can often settle these disputes either by royal decree ("It's my game, and that's how I'm going to play it") or by some compromise ("If we do it that way for your character, then my monster gets the same benefit"). Oftentimes, these decrees can leave various players upset with the DM or with other players and can create underlying strife in the group that leads to other conflicts.

Oftentimes, because the strife is too much, gamers choose to leave a group rather than adventure on. One group I played with was only marginally making it as a game. We had not switched into people who enjoyed each other's company, which was surprising given that two of the players were married. It all came to a head one day, though, when the husband had to roll a D20 to avoid his sword being broken or his character defending himself, I forget which. His wife, who was new to the game, said the unthinkable: "Roll a 1!" He threw down his hands and threatened to divorce her if he rolled a 1. And, of course...

Great *D&D* groups (and great marriages) do not form overnight.

WANTED

Adventurers to Investigate the *Perfectly Safe House* up
the Road where All the Maidens Keep Disappearing

A group of adventurers does not coalesce into a group of fast
friends over night. We all know the standard trope for any gaming group. We meet randomly in some village or city looking for
adventure and answer a call: a poster wanting hired adventurers, a mayor or prince seeking someone to rescue his missing
daughter/gold/magic ring, or a wizard looking for protection as
he goes to examine the dark ruins of some long-lost kingdom.
Our characters have never met, but we willingly join each other
for the gold held out in payment. Our characters often do not
trust each other at first: the elves mistrust the dwarves, who mistrust the goblin, and the paladin only barely trusts the cleric.
And no one trusts the poor burglar, who in turn trusts no one
else and has all of his goods tied down and hidden amongst his
baggage.

The rogue holds an interesting position in this group. If the
person playing the rogue is new to the gaming group, no one
knows exactly how she plays her rogue – whether she willingly
steals from other player-characters, whether she turns and runs
in a battle, or whether she will stab someone in the back for a
jewel. Likewise, the characters do not trust anyone dressed in
leather, carrying a dagger and not much else in weapons, and all
too quiet on her feet. The player and the player-character rogue
represent the embodiment of Aristotle's friend of utility. No one
wants a rogue around, but everyone needs a good rogue.

Our characters mirror the heroes of our favorite fantasy
novels. In *The Lord of the Rings*, Gimli and Legolas do not trust
each other when they meet in Rivendell, and Boromir has little
time for Aragorn. No one knows what to make of the hobbits.
The Fellowship of the Ring is not a fellowship until Gandalf has
fallen in Moria, Boromir has died with a thousand arrows in
him, and Frodo has escaped to desolate lands. Before then,
Boromir joins the group only because they are headed in the

general direction of Gondor, and he tries his best to convince
Frodo to use the ring in Gondor. In *The Princess Bride*, our
heroes start out as enemies and only become friends through a
need for each other to defeat the Prince and the Six-Fingered
Man. The same happens in every Shannara novel: a group of
people, brought together by a druid, begin a quest for a sword,
some elf stones, some forbidden knowledge. They do not know
each other beforehand, but they come to trust in each other as
the story progresses. The druid sets them up as friends of utility,
and we see right away that frustration mars their relationship.
Many epic fantasies are tales of individuals who start out as
friends of utility and turn into true friends. Just as many *D&D*
groups begin as friends of utility, and, if fortune is with them,
become true friends. Before that happens, though, they first
become friends of pleasure.

"Someone pass the Mountain Dew"

*Four of us huddled in the stairway during lunch break.
I played a paladin; I don't remember what the others were
playing any more.*

    *"So you've captured an orc. What do you do now?" the
DM asked.*

    "How many of you are there?" my paladin asked.

    "The orc spits in your face."

    Everyone laughs. Well, everyone except for me.

    *"Okay," Jamie says. "I take out my rope of climbing and
tie my dagger to it. Then I put the point right at his anus."*

I can't remember exactly, but I'm sure my paladin objected. I might
have been too stunned for my paladin to react. For years, I lost
track of Jamie, but I always remembered that scene. Even today,
when I communicate with "Jamison" on Facebook about
something Marx said, or some argument or other over property
or virtue or whatever, I remember him as Jamie, the rope-of-
climbing trickster. I would never have thought of Jamie as a

good friend back then, but I certainly took pleasure in his company, and, presumably he did in mine as well since we continued to game together the rest of that year.

We had reached, as many gaming groups do, a different stage of friendship – friends of pleasure. Friendships of pleasure involve friends who receive something similar from each other. *D&D* gamers receive the same kind of pleasure from each other – a love of *Dungeons & Dragons*, good role-playing, a shared idea about the right amount of role-playing versus hack-n-slash gaming. They enjoy the roll of the dice and the fact that they can come together and be someone different. They remain together because they receive pleasure from one another's gaming. "Those who love on account of pleasure feel affection for the sake of their own pleasure" (1156a16).

Once a *D&D* group has reached this level of friendship, division becomes less common. "There are also not many accusations in the friendships based on pleasure either, since both parties come to possess simultaneously what they long for, if they delight in going through life together" (1162b13–15). At this point, most rules-arguments have been settled. The players have established a routine, and know who is going to show up on time and who will show up late, who will bring what kind of snacks to share, and what everyone likes on their pizza. The DM has hit his stride and tries to work in something for each player-character in the game.

At the same time, the characters are getting along better as well. They have established watch cycles, they know who's going to go into the dungeon first, and they know who the weakest and strongest members are so that they can work together to beat the necromancer or vampire (we're not quite up to dragon-hunting yet). They can even gain a little pleasure from what each does in the game.

One time, Torodemo, my ranger, was being questioned by the bad guys – at that point in the game, nameless people who'd kidnapped him – about what he'd been doing and where he was going. Torodemo said, "I was visiting a girl with breasts like those mountains over there – firm and high." The kidnappers laughed.

Another time, Savros, another ranger (I'd long since left behind paladins and other refined goody-two-shoes), wanted to impress Ariel, a cleric who was leading our group – two paladins, a sorcerer, and Savros. He went into the woods, hunted down a mighty deer, skinned it, cleaned the skin, and brought the skin back to the church where we were staying. When Ariel came out, he bowed to her and handed her the deerskin. The paladins guffawed at the gesture, at the same time taken aback by the fresh deerskin. Our character personas, if we are truly role-playing, develop their own attitudes, likes, and dislikes. We play these out in the game in ways that might mirror or might differ completely from how we would act in real life. The point is that the characters develop relationships that mirror the relationships we develop with other players.

The Crusty Dagger: Food and Ale

In the *Lord of the Rings*, the friendship of Gimli and Legolas evolves from one of utility to one of pleasure. In the mines of Moria, Gimli waxes loquacious about the beauty of the mountain, and in Lothlorien, Legolas talks of the wonder and beauty of such forests. They agree that if they survive, they will each take the other to see some of the best caves and forests in Middle Earth. In *The Princess Bride*, Fezzik and Inigo Montoya play a game of rhyming words. In part, this game is to help Fezzik remember things, but it also brings the two together in wordplay that lays the foundation for a greater friendship to develop. The foundation of the *Symphony of Ages* series (by Elizabeth Haydon) is based on a friendship of pleasure – two teenagers, Gwydion and Emily, are thrust together for a night, fall passionately in love, and then lose each other through some mysterious person's manipulation of time. Much of the first three books of the series focuses on their attempt to reunite in a distant land a thousand years in the future of their world. As a final example, in *A Game of Thrones*, Eddard Stark, on becoming Hand to King Robert Baratheon, is both maddened by and delightfully reminiscent of Robert's love of food and the hunt. Robert wants to have by his side someone he used to do pleasurable things with when younger before being king – hunting, drinking and carousing, and fighting. This pleasure cements both Eddard's loyalty to Robert and his eventual beheading.

Gimli and Legolas, on the one hand, and Eddard Stark and Robert Baratheon, on the other, testify to some of what Aristotle says about friends of pleasure and true friends. All friendship, for Aristotle, requires some equality. Gimli and Legolas are equal in that they voluntarily join the Fellowship of the Ring to guide Frodo as far as he will let them. Originally, they gain something from each other in equal parts – a companion on the road, another sword in a fight, and a sharing of the burden of caring for Frodo. Eventually, their equality becomes richer, as they begin to share a love for forests, when they first enter Lothlorien. Legolas is superior in his knowledge of forests, but he wants to make Gimli love them equally. In the first instance, Aristotle would see a friendship of utility, and in the second, a friendship of pleasure.

Robert Baratheon and Eddard Stark are not equal – Robert is king and demands that Eddard return to King's Landing. Yet Robert tries to treat Eddard as an equal once they've returned – he wants his old hunting buddy back. Yet the reader sees in that desire a stark difference in moral virtue between Robert and Eddard. Robert has no time, patience, or desire to rule his kingdom. He does not perform his duty. Eddard, on the other hand, follows Robert out of a sense of duty. He is the more virtuous of the two. On that basis, Aristotle would contend that Robert and Eddard could never be true friends – even if they once were. True friendship occurs between those who are equally virtuous and love the good. The reader sees Eddard reflect on this very fact a number of times as he waits for Robert to perform some duty necessary to keep the kingdom running, and he laments the Robert he used to know. In contrast, Robert's tomfoolery gets him gored by a boar, and Eddard's loyalty gets him executed by Robert's son.

Interestingly enough, one reason Aristotle believes people need friends is that only through friendship can one exercise certain virtues that are necessary for leading a flourishing life. One such virtue is loyalty. Gimli and Legolas show a fierce loyalty, at first to their own people (for they join the Fellowship as representatives of their people), secondly to Frodo, and finally to each other. Eddard shows a strong loyalty to Robert, but Robert is incapable of loyalty. He no longer lives a life of virtue, and thus he cannot achieve flourishing. He can only live a life of pleasure, from which he dies. Eddard believes he is flourishing, but because of his own loyalty he cannot see the deception plotted by Littlefinger (despite the fact that it's written on the stars for the rest of us). Bereft of friends and surrounded by base people, Eddard becomes a tragic hero whose flaw is loyalty itself. For Aristotle, the flaw rests in the lack of friendship. Loyalty is a virtue only for true friends – that is, those who are virtuous – and not something to be given to those who are base.

In our *D&D* games, our characters likewise will remain merely friends of utility or friends of pleasure unless they share equally in virtue and value the good life. No one thinks that the paladin and the rogue can become true friends, and often the ideas about the good that the druid has conflict too much with those of the dwarven fighters. Still, friends of pleasure prove necessary for life because everyone desires pleasure.

"The friendship of those who are good then, is friendship most of all"

The morning sun gleamed off the paladins' armor. Savros had killed the king of the were-rats with their help, but greater trouble was brewing.

"It's our old master. He has turned to evil, and we need help stopping him," Henri said.

Ariel was nowhere around, but I knew she would be helping. They were her knights after all. Still, I didn't belong here. I was thousands of miles from home, a home that needed rebuilding after the army of were-rats had gone through destroying everything, killing everyone, including my parents. I'd been gone for over a year.

Kronin shifted, his armor rattling. I shook my head. How many times had I cursed these paladins and their loud armor when I was quietly preparing to ambush someone? Still, I'd grown to care for them. They were not family, but they were brothers. And we might not agree exactly on methods – what use is law when marauders kill everything in their path? Yet, we loved the same things: Ariel, first of all, but peace and justice too.

I nodded. "I will be there with you."

Aristotle said that "there is also need of passage of time and the habits formed by living together, for as the adage has it, it is not possible for people to know each other until they have eaten together of the proverbial salt, nor is it possible, before this occurs, for them to accept each other and to be friends until each appears as lovable and is trusted" (1156b26–29).

When players play together long enough, their characters pass through a variety of adventures. Good role-playing allows the characters to develop attachments, not only to the other characters, but to their individual quests. They have indeed eaten of the proverbial salt together by fighting the same enemy. They did not start out for the same reasons: some wanted fame, others gold, others to serve their god. Yet as the story in the game progressed, so did their interest in the world of the game and the good and evil as seen by each other. They come to share some understanding of what the game-world is like.

They do not do this overnight or even after a few months of gaming. It takes some time. Players need a chance to share the troubles of their everyday lives with the others around the gaming table. Experienced gamers know that the game doesn't start when all the players show up. First, players shoot the breeze and talk about their week. Now, after playing together for a long time, they want to know what's going on in their lives: what trouble they're having in a class, or the new girl or guy someone is dating, or how the interview went last week. This sort of debriefing is a sign that the players are on the verge of true friendship brought about through sharing the proverbial salt.

True friendships, however, develop only rarely: "Yet friendships of this sort are likely to be rare, since people of this sort are few" (1156b25). What sort of people? Aristotle believes that only good people can become true friends: "But a good person is lovable and choiceworthy" (1157b29) both because she truly is good and pleasant in an unqualified sense and because she is good and pleasant to the friend. Anyone who is good enjoys being around someone else who is truly good – virtuous and flourishing. That virtuous and flourishing person is good and pleasant, and so choiceworthy in herself and not simply for some advantage or pleasure she brings. Yet the virtuous and flourishing person is good and pleasant to the friend. That is, not only is such a person choiceworthy in herself, but she does good things and is pleasing to her friends. Savros found Henri and Kronin both good people and valued them simply because they were good, regardless of any benefit they brought to him – saving his life sometimes. Yet he also valued them because they were good to him – helping him find ways to impress Ariel – and were pleasant to him – inviting him to join them in a drink or two.

When we are lucky, the people we game with can become true friends in this way. We value other gamers not simply because they are good to us – offering rides to a game or letting us slide on paying for pizza some week, or helping us move. We also value them occasionally because we think they are good people, people that we think the world needs more of. Such friendships do not develop with every gamer. We have to discover that the other gamer is someone who is good – which means someone we see as equal in virtue to ourselves. They have to be equal in virtue to us because the reason we think the world needs more people like them is that they are virtuous. Further, if we are not virtuous ourselves, we are unlikely to find them valuable in themselves.

I met Brandon in grad school. He was a year ahead of me, so we didn't attend the same classes. We managed to hang out and be friendly to each other, though. Then, we started gaming together – at first with Chris and Pam. Pam moved on, leaving grad school, but Ben took her place. For a period of three years, we were more than friends of utility or pleasure – we were true friends who valued philosophy most of all, but also valued *Dungeons & Dragons*, discussed justice, and supported each other in our struggles writing our dissertations. Had it not been for *D&D*, we would never have been as close. *D&D* brought us together once a week, and we were able to talk about the most important things in our lives. This encouraged us to find other reasons to be together – movies mainly, but also philosophy lectures and the philosophy graduate student association meetings.

In finding a true friend we are in fact finding another self. "For such people wish in similar fashion for the good things for each other insofar as they are good, and they are good in themselves. But those who wish for the good things for their friends, for their friends' sake, are friends most of all, since they are disposed in this way in themselves and not incidentally" (1156b10–12). We want our true friends to have the best in the world – that is, what is truly good, a career in which they flourish, a spouse/partner with whom they share happiness and burdens equally, healthy and good children, and all those little things that add a little joy to our lives.

I've stayed in fairly constant contact with Brandon since grad school, and only sporadic contact with Ben and Chris. I can't explain why, except perhaps that Brandon and I were similar. We are both from Kentucky and both worked under the same dissertation director concerned with topics that were related to each other (whereas Chris and Ben worked on topics not quite in the same sub-field as ours and under different directors). Today, Brandon is trying his hand at writing urban fantasy, which I had tried once long ago. The point of course is not to say what great friends I have, but to say that *D&D* brought us together in way that other things might not have. Through *Dungeons & Dragons*, we forged a friendship of shared values and shared meanings – which is the very definition of true friendship for Aristotle.

"I'm glad you're with me now at the end of all things"

In the *Lord of the Rings*, Gimli and Legolas become true friends. They are equally brave in the battles that rage through *The Two Towers* and *The Return of the King*. More importantly, they wish for each other to be victorious in battle, and they wish to spend their lives together traveling Middle Earth after Aragorn has taken his throne in Gondor. Likewise Samwise Gamgee moves in with his master, Frodo Baggins. It is difficult for us readers to imagine that the heroes of our fantasy novels go their separate ways in the end. We expect them to want to be together because of the friendships they've formed. According to Aristotle, our desire here recognizes an important element of true friendship: "For since they wish to live with their friends, they pursue and share in those things in which they suppose living together consists" (1172a7–8).

At the end of *Rhapsody: Child of Blood* (in the *Symphony of Ages* series), Grunthor and Achmed build a small place for Rhapsody to live in within their mountain kingdom. They have spent a thousand years together traveling through the center of the world to reach their new home. At first, Achmed wanted to kill Rhapsody, but through their trials and tribulations they became friends of pleasure and then true friends who cared about the world. One thing they share is a concern for educating the Firbolg (a race of barbarian half-giants), a concern to prevent the darkness that seems to be threatening their new home, and a love for each other. They have grown from originally selfish desires to something deeper.

"Since friendship consists more in loving than in being loved, those who love their friends are praised, loving seems to be a virtue of friends" (1159a4–5). Achmed, Grunthor, and Rhapsody, Sam and Frodo, Legolas and Gimli all share the virtue of love, which is a virtue particular to true friendship. For Aristotle, one lives a flourishing life by living virtuously. Virtues help one to control one's desires and passions, and thus act voluntarily to pursue what is truly good. Because true friendships form between good people, having good friends constitutes, in part, the good which people pursue. Such people are good in themselves and choiceworthy for who they are. Sam loves Frodo because of who Frodo is and for no other reason. His love has nothing to do with the fact that Frodo owns Bag-end or carried the One Ring to Mount Doom. Legolas loves Gimli for who he is – a dwarf of virtue and goodness. Rhapsody loves Grunthor and Achmed because she sees their true good – their dedication to eradicate evil, despite the fact that they claim otherwise.

Just as friendships of utility and friendships of pleasure can transform in the fantasy novel to true friendships, so likewise, those who begin playing *D&D* as friends of utility or pleasure can transform into true friends who care for each other through thick and thin. I would argue that *Dungeons & Dragons* functions as a practice that allows such friendships to develop. A practice is "any coherent and complex form of socially established cooperative human activity through which goods internal to that form of activity are realized in the course of trying to achieve those standards of excellence which are appropriate to, and partially definitive of, that form of activity, with the result that human powers to achieve excellence, and the human conceptions of the ends and goods involved, are systematically extended."[2] In short, a practice is a set of activities that allows people to seek the good together and develop their virtues.[3]

In arguing that *D&D* comprises a practice in which individuals learn the virtues and pursue the good, I do not mean to say that everyone who plays *D&D* will become a virtuous, flourishing individual, just as I would not say that everyone who enters the army becomes brave, or that everyone who has a family becomes a great parent. Rather, I mean that *D&D* can be one of those things through which people develop a variety of virtues, especially loyalty and love, and learn a little bit about what the flourishing human life involves. *D&D* players know a lot about friendship and the value of friendship in a person's life, despite the popular depiction of gamers. Through *D&D*, individuals have the opportunity not only to learn about friendship, loyalty, and love, but also to develop those rare true friendships in which they live a life valuing loyalty and love.

Notes

1. "Others play at dice…each passing their days together in whatever they are fondest of" (*Nicomachean Ethics*, 1172a5–6). All quotes, except where otherwise noted, are from Aristotle, *Nicomachean Ethics*, trans. Robert C. Bartlett and Susan D. Collins (Chicago: University Of Chicago Press, 2012). Page and line references are to the standard Bekker translation of 1831 and are included in text.
2. Alasdair MacIntyre, *After Virtue* (Notre Dame: University of Notre Dame Press, 1984), p. 187.
3. "Eucharist and Dragon Fighting as Resistance: Against Commodity Fetishism and Scientism," *Philosophy and Management* 7 (2008), pp. 93–106.

Contributors

Ashley Brown is currently based in the Sociology Department at the University of Manchester, UK. Although she used to consider herself a true neutral druid of the grove, recent conversations with co-author Matt Jones have caused an alignment drop to neutral evil. Although there are some downsides, she has to admit that raising the dead to do her bidding has certainly increased productivity.

Rob Crandall lives and games in Madison, Wisconsin – for a generous definition of "lives." As the latest mortal guise of a centuries-old arch-lich, his foul ambition is matched only by his delight in abusing multiclass rules. When not weaving unspeakable plots, he spends his days researching lost magic, maintaining his army of minions, and tempting adventurers with promises of dark power. He spends his nights trying to get enough rest to recover his spell slots.

Robert A. Delfino is Associate Professor of Philosophy at St. John's University, New York. He received his PhD from SUNY Buffalo, where he specialized in metaphysics and medieval philosophy. His current research interests include the relationship between science and religion, the metaphysical foundations of ethics, and the nature of the soul. In the fifth grade he was lucky to sit next

Dungeons & Dragons and Philosophy: Read and Gain Advantage on All Wisdom Checks, First Edition. Edited by Christopher Robichaud.
© 2014 John Wiley & Sons, Inc. Published 2014 by John Wiley & Sons, Inc.

to Jerome Hillock, who introduced him to *D&D* and many years of great friendship and adventure. There are days when he would prefer to live in Rivendell, spending nights drinking ale and mead while laughing with old friends.

Ben Dyer has taken several levels in moral and political philosophy, and has recently begun multi-classing in instructional design. A lawful-good philosopher, he quests in search of truth, justice, and warm feelings of moral superiority, knowing full well that he may never find truth and justice. He is also a conscientious objector to the edition wars whose tabletop tastes are ecumenical, frequently eccentric, and liable to tinkering given world enough and time.

Karington Hess is one of the innkeepers at Ravenwood Castle. Tales of his exploits are well known in the gilded city of Quincy, Illinois. Recently he has traveled to the faraway land of Ohio in search of new adventures and excitement. In his current role as innkeeper, he tends to the needs of the wary travelers who bravely venture in to the perilous reaches of southeastern Ohio. He enjoys the many tales of treasure, heroism, magic, and the good life told to him by other adventurers. He has a tale or two himself to tell already, but as he looks at his old bag of holding, he wonders … Is he ready for his next adventure?

Jerome C. Hillock received his BA in English literature from Rutgers University. It was 1982 on Staten Island, NY, when he was first introduced to *AD&D* by his elder brother, Charlie. It was not a direct indoctrination, but rather consisted of raids of his brother's room the next morning for Entenmann's chocolate chip cookies where he would peruse the painted metal figurines and read the obscure manuals left there. Jerome felt impelled to anoint himself with the mantle of Dungeon Master and imposed his esteemed title on his fifth-grade desk partner Robert Delfino. A year later, his role was officiated through the mail in receipt of a dozen pencils from Honey Nut Cheerio emblazoned "The DM

Rules!" Jerome is credited in the financial industry with starting the trend of assigning all clients in terms of strength, intelligence, wisdom, dexterity, constitution, and charisma on a 3–18 scale. Jerome can be found on the weekends evangelizing with his deities and demigods, first edition, which includes Cthulhu and Melnibonean gods. His main Dungeon Mastering continues with his 4-year-old son, where he teaches him how to get along with NPCs.

Matt Hummel, after venturing north to become a Master of Arts in ethics and values at Valparaiso University, returned to his homeland in Evansville, Indiana. There he serves as a second-level apprentice to the dark wizards commonly referred to as "defense attorneys." In exchange for tutelage in the mystical and all but incomprehensible sorcery that is American criminal law, he gives the "lawyers" lessons in shapeshifting, helping them seem almost human as they advocate for those accused of being wicked. Word has it Matt will soon adjunct at the Academy of the Underdark to instruct new generations in the backward morality of drow society.

Matthew Jones is a doctoral student writing on the political and religious thought of Thomas Hobbes. Reports that he is either lawful evil in alignment or affiliated in any way with the cults of Orcus or Chemosh are greatly exaggerated.

The Hand and Eye of **Greg Littmann** are cursed artifacts. If a character removes an eye and replaces it with the Eye of Greg Littmann, they will become Associate Professor of Philosophy at SIUE. If they amputate their hand and attach the Hand to the stump, they will publish on metaphilosophy, metaphysics and philosophy of logic, and will write more than twenty-five chapters for books relating philosophy to popular culture, including volumes on *Adventure Time*, *Big Bang Theory*, *Doctor Who*, *Final Fantasy*, *Game of Thrones*, *The Walking Dead*, Neil Gaiman, and Roald Dahl. A character who attaches both the Eye and Hand will contract septicemia.

Esther MacCallum-Stewart has been spending weekends in muddy fields waving swords or drinking bad wine in bedsits whilst rolling for initiative for most of her life. She spent her first live action role-playing event lying in a bramble bush because the party hadn't noticed she was dead (hey, it was dark, okay!), but didn't let it put her off and has been pulling thorns out of her cloaks ever since. Esther has been role-playing with a group of friends for over twenty years, where they have seen betrayal, love on the Reik, and far too many voluminous muffs for comfort. She has an unconscionable fondness for dwarves (och, they're nice), and prides herself on her collection of lovely, lovely dice. Esther is also a Research Fellow at the Digital Cultures Research Centre and a Senior Lecturer at the University of Surrey, UK. Her work examines the ways that players understanding gaming narratives, and she has written widely on role-playing, gender, deviant play, and gaming communities.

Kevin McCain is an Assistant Professor of Philosophy at the University of Alabama at Birmingham. He is a master of the sneak attack and superb at hurling well-placed fireballs. But, he is most sought after for his dice-rolling skills and his ability to pass the potato chips during the surprise round of combat. It is for these reasons that his name is spoken in hushed whispers around gaming tables the world over.

J.K. Miles is Assistant Professor of Philosophy at Quincy University. He has been rolling dice since he was knee high to a kobold and cut his teeth on the first printing of *AD&D*. He favors the rogue class and thinks paladins make great meat shields. His love of medieval and Renaissance life led him to join the Society for Creative Anachronism so he could poke people with a sword for real, though he was disappointed they didn't allow sneak attacks. Occasionally he can be found quaffing potions of wisdom to help with his philosophy research and figuring out ways to work discussions of Marvel Comics into his ethics lectures.

Neil Mussett, using second edition rules, switched classes from graduate-level philosopher to first-level programmer. He has advanced to one level higher than his previous philosopher class and is now able to use those abilities (although he can never advance as a philosopher). He aspires one day to make sense of the rules around Psionic Powers.

Shannon M. Mussett is Associate Professor of Philosophy and chair of the Department of Philosophy and Humanities at Utah Valley University. After a childhood spent playing *D&D*, drawing unicorns, and reading fantasy novels, she decided to grow up and become a professor of philosophy where she basically gets paid to do the same thing.

Jeffery L. Nicholas went to school to be a bard, but was misled by a cleric and ended up being a wizard (of philosophy), which is fine since he doesn't have charisma anyway and at least didn't end up a cleric. His backpack contains several scrolls of pop culture and philosophy: one in *The Big Lebowski and Philosophy* and one in *Ender's Game and Philosophy*. He also penned a tome on reason … mainly because he failed an intelligence check once. The wizarding life has caused Jeff to move his family across the great land of "America" twice, but now he resides in the poorly named Rhode Island where he teaches ethics at Providence College.

Samantha Noll is a doctoral student in philosophy of science and animal ethics at Michigan State University. She's been an avid *Dungeons & Dragons* player since the tender age of 8, when she saved up her allowance money to buy her first Dungeon Master's Guide. At that time, she could occasionally be caught wearing a wizarding robe, using her staff to dispel demons (aka her brothers) from her plane of existence (aka her room). Today, while her wizarding robe and staff are largely lost in the attic crypt, it is whispered in dark alleys that goblins should take care, as you never know when they might surface again … to the chagrin of her spouse.

Christopher Robichaud is Lecturer in Ethics and Public Policy at the Harvard Kennedy School of Government. He's been rolling D20s for over three decades and shows no signs of stopping. He'd like to give a shout-out to his weekly group at Pandemonium Books and Games in Central Square, Cambridge, Massachusetts. Young and old alike, his players tolerate him brutalizing their characters with glee in the deadly dungeon crawls he runs. A Dungeon Master at heart, Christopher never gained the evil superpowers that the 1980s promised him he was going to get from playing the game, but that's never kept him from enjoying it all the same.

Charles Taliaferro (neutral good human cleric) teaches philosophy and religion at St. Olaf College, where his auxiliary responsibilities include protecting the campus from the undead. After he was gravely injured in a quest to recover a copy of the Book of Exalted Deeds from Nessus he was forced to retire from active adventuring, but he keeps his holy symbol polished and ready in case his god calls upon him to once more face the forces of evil. He enjoys vacations on Arborea, although he wishes the eladrin would turn the music down.

William J. White is Associate Professor of Communication Arts & Sciences at Penn State Altoona. His players assure him that a PhD in communication has improved his dungeon mastering skills immensely. He is particularly proud of his Campbellian random adventure generator, "The Hero with 1d1000 Faces," which appeared in Dragon #274. More recently, his noirish Lovecraftian RPG scenario, "The Big Hoodoo," in which the player-characters are sci-fi authors Bob Heinlein, Phil Dick, and Tony Boucher investigating the death by explosion of rocket scientist occultist Jack Parsons in 1952 Pasadena (published by Pelgrane Press in a collection called *Out of Time*), was declared by one critic to be "an excellent example of hitting what you're aiming at." If you ask him nicely, he'll probably come run a game for you and your friends.

Index

Fictional characters are entered under their first name; for example, Raistlin Majere appears under R.

*Dungeons & Dragons and Philosophy: Read and Gain Advantage
on All Wisdom Checks*, First Edition. Edited by Christopher Robichaud.
© 2014 John Wiley & Sons, Inc. Published 2014 by John Wiley & Sons, Inc.

Printed and bound by CPI Group (UK) Ltd, Croydon, CR0 4YY

25/03/2025

14647358-0001